# THE REAL BRAVO TWO ZERO

# THE REAL
# BRAVO TWO ZERO

## THE TRUTH BEHIND BRAVO TWO ZERO

Michael Asher

CASSELL&CO

Cassell & Co
Wellington House, 125 Strand
London WC2R 0BB

Copyright © Michael Asher 2002

First published 2002

British Library Cataloguing-in-Publication data:
A catalogue record for this book is available from the
British Library

ISBN 0-304-36369-3

Printed and bound in Great Britain by
MPG Books Ltd, Bodmin, Cornwall

For Richard Belfield,

Fulcrum TV's visionary Producer
who thought of it, and had the courage and faith to
see it through:

MAGNA EST VERITAS ET PRAEVALEBIT

# CONTENTS

# LIST OF ILLUSTRATIONS

*between pp126-127*

Michael Asher on the trail of Bravo Two Zero. *Jon Lane*

The LUP (Lying-Up Position) where Bravo Two Zero patrol was  compromised. *Owen Scurfield*

Abbas bin Fadhil. *Owen Scurfield*

Abbas's family. *Owen Scurfield*

Michael and Nigel Morris with their military escort. *Owen Scurfield*

The bulldozer from which Abbas bin Fadhil spotted the patrol. *Channel 4*

The taxi hijacked by Andy McNab. *Jon Lane*

Hayil, Mohammed, Abbas, Michael and Adil (the shepherd boy whom McNab and Ryan say compromised Bravo Two Zero). *Owen Scurfield*

The pump-house where the dying Legs Lane was captured. *Jon Lane*

Michael with one of the Minimi 5.56mm machine-guns captured by the Iraqis from Bravo Two Zero. *Owen Scurfield*

The field where Mike Coburn was captured by the Iraqis. *Channel 4*

Vince Phillips's binoculars. *Channel 4*

Where Andy McNab was captured. *Channel 4*

Michael, Ahmad the policeman and Subhi the lawyer, on the spot where Bob Consiglio was shot and killed by armed civilians. *Jon Lane*

Michael and Mohammed stand by Vince's cairn. *Jon Lane*

# ACKNOWLEDGEMENTS

I would like to thank the following :

Jeff, Steve and Veronica Phillips and their families. Major Peter Ratcliffe DCM. Abbas bin Fadhil, Hayil bin Fadhil and all those Iraqis who contributed to the film. Charles Furneaux of Channel 4. The management and staff at Fulcrum TV: Christopher Hird, Beth Holgate, Martin Long, Annie Moore, Donna Blackburn, and everyone else who worked on the film. The film crew in Iraq, including Gavin Searle (Director), Jon Lane and Owen Scurfield (camera crew) and Nigel Morris (Associate Producer). Ian Drury, Publishing Director at Orion Books. Anthony Goff and Georgia Glover of David Higham Associates, my agents. A special thanks to my wife, Mariantonietta, an Arabic translator, for her deep translation of Adnan Badawi's article, which revealed interesting new insights. Lastly, my children, Burton and Jade.

# INTRODUCTION

IN THE GREAT BRITISH tradition it was a glorious failure. Almost everything that could go wrong did. On 22 January 1991 – five days into the ground phase of the Gulf War – a patrol of 22 SAS was inserted deep behind enemy lines in the desert of Iraq. The eight-strong team had been tasked to help find the Scud missiles whose deployment against Israel by Saddam Hussein was jeopardizing the fragile Coalition. The story of what happened has become the stuff of legend. Compromised on the second day, unable to contact their base or use their emergency beacons, the patrol was attacked and split up. Following a farrago of mistakes, failures and sheer bad luck, three of the team died and four were captured. Only one managed to escape, in a near-suicidal trek to the Syrian border.

Bravo Two Zero, called the most decorated British patrol since the Boer War, has already found a place beside the likes of Lawrence

of Arabia in modern military folklore. The most written-about, reported-on and debated incident in the history of Special Operations, it owes its fame mainly to the books published by two of its members, *Bravo Two Zero,* by the patrol commander, who writes under the alias 'Andy McNab' and *The One That Got Away* by the escapee, alias 'Chris Ryan'. These books have enjoyed phenomenal success; both became massive bestsellers with combined sales in excess of three million. McNab's book, presented as 'The true story of an SAS patrol behind enemy lines in Iraq', was hailed by James Adams of the *Sunday Times* as 'the best account yet of the SAS in action', while *Soldier Magazine* declared that Ryan's book must 'rank with the great escape stories of modern military history'. Both books have been turned into TV dramatizations and translated into many languages, ensuring that the fame of Bravo Two Zero has reached tens of millions of people worldwide. Ryan and McNab, who both went on to become writers of bestselling fiction, are probably the only major national British military heroes to have emerged in modern times. The saga of the Bravo Two Zero patrol has become a modern Charge of the Light Brigade and the blame for its failure has been placed in various quarters. McNab names the SAS hierarchy and intelligence sector, evoking the *Bridge Too Far* blunder at Arnhem by saying that the patrol was dropped in an area where 'there were more than 3000 Iraqi troops . . . effectively two armoured brigades that shouldn't have been there, that intelligence hadn't picked up'.[1] He also says that the patrol was put into the field without reference to the fundamentals of military practice – what he calls the Seven Ps: Proper Prior Planning Prevents Piss Poor Performance. He says the patrol had no accurate maps, aerial photos or satellite images, were not given the correct

radio frequencies, were not instructed to take cold-weather clothing or sleeping-bags, were not informed that the ground would be rocky rather than sandy, or even that the weather would be remarkably cold.

A third member of the patrol, who writes as 'Mike Coburn', but is referred to in the other books as 'Mark', has said recently that the RAF dropped them in the wrong place, and that the 'Head Shed' betrayed them by failing to send out an immediate rescue mission, but the blame for what went wrong is not laid solely on the Regimental hierarchy. One of the patrol members in particular – the dead Sergeant Vince Phillips – is vilified, particularly by Ryan, as the Jonas behind many of the unit's misfortunes. According to Ryan, Phillips, the 2i/c (second-in-command) of the patrol, was incompetent, unprofessional and even cowardly. Writing that Phillips was nervous and twitchy before the operation, he says that the sergeant resented having to be there, and was anxious just to serve out the rest of his time in the army in peace. Ryan also writes that on the ground Phillips was negative and indecisive, accuses him of falling asleep on stag (sentry duty), and blames him squarely for compromising the patrol. Though McNab is by far the less scathing of the two, he hints that Phillips was responsible for the patrol splitting by failing to pass on a message, which, he writes, did not penetrate the sergeant's 'numbed brain'.

Although I was impressed by both books on first reading, I was left with a nagging feeling that something was wrong. If the Head Shed was truly as inept as both authors made out, and if their own colleague, Vince Phillips, was really incompetent, then the Regiment's very excellence was being brought into question.

Like most who have served in the SAS family, I firmly believe

that the Regiment is the finest fighting unit in the world. The best day of my life was the day I was presented with the buff-coloured beret of the SAS. I had just completed selection for 23 SAS, one of the Regiment's two territorial units, and was immensely proud of what I had achieved. I still am. Like selection for 22 SAS, the regular unit, TA selection involves months of back-breaking legwork and culminates in a gruelling fortnight in the Brecon Beacons, with an overall attrition rate of ninety per cent. For me the toil was infinitely worthwhile, because I believe that the SAS beret symbolizes something rather rare in our society. It cannot be bought, inherited, or acquired by privilege. It has to be earned. I have served as a regular soldier in the Parachute Regiment and in the police Special Patrol Group anti-terrorist squad, but the sense of pride I felt that day on being initiated into the SAS remains unique.

Three years after passing selection for 23 SAS, I left Britain to become a volunteer teacher in a remote region of the Sudan. There I learned to speak Arabic and to handle a camel, and became so engrossed in Arab culture that I eventually gave up teaching to live with a traditional Bedouin tribe. These people, the Kababish, hardly belonged to the twentieth century at all. Owning no modern technology, no cars, TVs or radios, most could not read or write, and had not travelled in a motor vehicle, and many had never been in a city. Oblivious to politics in their own country, and often unaware even of the name of their own president, they lived an itinerant life unchanged for generations, moving their camels and goats from place to place in search of pasture and water. They lived in black tents and carried their entire world on their camels' backs, their rifles always in their hands, ready to repel raiders. The most interesting aspect of their culture was the fact that people were never judged by what they

owned. The most respected man was not the richest, but the one most endowed with the quality of 'human-ness' – a combination of courage, endurance, hospitality, generosity and loyalty. Among the Bedouin, a man's word is his bond, and lying is considered the ultimate disgrace. The three years I spent living with the Bedouin were not only the most fascinating years of my life, but they also gave me a deep affection and respect for these desert nomads that I have never lost.

I also learned a great deal from them that I was able to put to good use later. In 1986-7, with my wife Mariantonietta, I made the first ever west-east crossing of the Sahara Desert by camel and on foot – a distance of 4500 miles – in nine months. I lived among the 'Fuzzy Wuzzies' – the Beja tribes of the eastern Sudan – and crossed the Great Sand Sea of Egypt by camel with a Bedouin companion. In twenty years I have covered almost twenty thousand miles across the world's deserts without the use of the internal combustion engine, and have lived and travelled with many nomadic peoples. It was the Regiment that prepared me for that, and I believe my life would have been very different without the lessons in determination, adaptability and resilience I learned with the SAS.

Since the Regiment's excellence is a crucial base-line in my own life, I was particularly unwilling to believe that Vince Phillips – a senior NCO (non-commissioned officer) in that unit – could have been as inadequate as he has been portrayed. Phillips was the most experienced soldier in the patrol. With twenty years' service under his belt, he had put in time with both the Parachute Brigade and the Commando Brigade before being accepted for the SAS. A champion army marathoner, he was also known for his outstanding physical fitness, and with nine years in the Regiment behind him, was more seasoned even than patrol commander McNab, let alone the relative newcomer

Ryan. If Vince Phillips did not know his job, then the jury has to be out on the selection process that lies at the heart of the Regiment's philosophy – a process that had been an important milestone for me.

There was another thing that bothered me about the portrayal of Phillips. Even in the event that what Ryan had written was correct, it is not in the Regiment's tradition to publicly slander a fallen comrade who has no means of answering back. After all, Vince did not 'beat the clock', as they say in the Regiment – he made the supreme sacrifice for Queen and country, leaving a widowed wife and two fatherless daughters. While both Ryan and McNab have made millions from their books, Vince has become notorious as 'the man who blew Bravo Two Zero', and his body lies forgotten in the Regimental graveyard, without even a posthumous medal to redeem it.

My quest to find out about Vince took me to the deserts of Iraq, where I was able to follow in the footsteps of the Bravo Two Zero patrol, the first Western writer to be allowed in that area since the Gulf War. Not only was I able to view the ground on which the action had taken place, but I was also able to interview at least ten eyewitnesses. Many of these were simple Bedouin or Fellahin, with no axe to grind or reason not to tell the truth. What I discovered astonished me. It presented a very different picture from the stories told in McNab's and Ryan's books – indeed, it differed in almost every significant detail. If what I found out was correct, then Vince had not compromised the patrol, had not been responsible for the split, and had not behaved in the cowardly way Ryan describes.

My research revealed, moreover, that the blame for what went wrong could not be laid at the door of the Regimental command – responsibility for much of the Bravo Two Zero debacle lay squarely with the decorated 'hero' of the patrol, 'Andy McNab' himself.

# CHAPTER
## one

IN APRIL 2001, JUST OVER ten years since Jeff Phillips was told that his brother Vince had died in Iraq, I visited him at his home in Swindon. Jeff was a stocky, quiet, unassuming man, his features recognizably from the same mould as those of the elder brother whose portrait stared down at me from the wall of the small sitting-room. The portrait confirmed McNab's description of Vince as a man who was every inch what a member of the public would expect an SAS man to look like: coarse, curly hair and sideboards and a curling moustache – McNab calls him 'a big old boy, immensely strong', who 'walked everywhere – even up hills – as if he had a barrel of beer under each arm'.[2] Jeff's home had become a sort of shrine to Vince and as well as the portrait, there were photos, an impressive array of books and videos on Special Forces subjects, albums of newspaper cuttings and memorabilia, SAS shields, a shamagh, and

even a ceramic plate with the winged-dagger crest. Jeff showed me Vince's SAS beret and stable-belt, bought and presented to him by a comrade of Vince's in the traditional 'dead man's auction'.

Jeff, himself a former platoon sergeant in the infantry, introduced me to his younger brother Steve and their mother Veronica, and as we talked it soon became clear that Vince had been a hero to the Phillips family: his service in the Regiment was a source of great pride. 'He was very fit,' Jeff said. 'He used to run marathons, and he often went out walking in the Beacons. He was always well prepared too, and used to warn us not to go up into the mountains without the proper kit. That's why we found it hard to believe when they told us he'd died of hypothermia. Dee (Vince's wife) had an official letter from the Commanding Officer of 22 SAS saying he thought he'd died of hypothermia on the night of 25/26 January 1991, and the inquest came to the same conclusion. But in fact we still don't know for sure what happened to him. Ryan maintains he just wandered off, so he never knew even if he was dead or alive, and in fact no one in the family ever saw him before he was buried. I took a pair of Vince's trainers down to Hereford before the funeral to put in the coffin, because Vince loved his marathons, but the MOD wouldn't let me in. They took the trainers, but wouldn't let me see his body. Dee was offered a chance to see him, but turned it down at the last moment – we don't know why. We have no idea what's in the coffin, or even if it's Vince at all. He might have been taken alive by the Iraqis, used as a human shield and blown to pieces for all we know.'

Worse than the mystery of what happened to Vince, Jeff told me, was the calumny that had been heaped upon his memory, particularly by Ryan. 'My father died of cancer quite recently,' he said, 'and I put his death down to his worries about Vince. He never got

over what Ryan said about him. It used to make him livid, and he was always writing letters to complain about the way he'd been portrayed. After the TV version of *The One That Got Away* came out, people used to come up to him at work and say, "Your son was the one who got Bravo Two Zero in the shit." You can imagine how that made him feel – to have your son, my brother, remembered all over the world as a bungler and a coward. It really affected Dad badly, and in fact when he died the doctor told us, "There goes another victim of the Gulf War."'

Ryan's main charge against Vince was that he was responsible for compromising the patrol when he moved and was spotted by a boy herding goats near their hiding place. Ryan says that Vince later admitted he had seen the boy, and concludes that in this case the boy must have seen Vince. 'I don't believe Vince was as nervous as Ryan said,' Jeff told me. 'Nor do I believe he compromised the patrol. He was far too professional for that.'

One of the worst blows to Vince's memory, though, came from a classified SAS report that had been leaked to the *Mail On Sunday*, concluding that Vince had been 'difficult to work with' and 'lacked the will to survive'. Alleging that 'his heart was simply not in the task', the report also accused him of falling asleep on watch and of 'compromising the operation by getting up and moving about when the others were hiding from a goatherd'. It was evident that the stain on Vince's honour had caused great pain and anguish to the Phillips family, so I wanted to find out for myself what really happened.


MONTHS EARLIER, WHEN RICHARD Belfield of Fulcrum TV and Charles Furneaux of Channel 4 had suggested that I should go

to Iraq with a film-crew to investigate what really happened, I'd been hesitant. For a start, there was still a war on in the country; with UN sanctions in place and US and British aircraft flying bombing sorties in the south, I didn't believe that the Iraqis would give me the time of day. Secondly, I still felt a sense of loyalty to the Regiment, and didn't want to be seen as engaged on some kind of debunking exercise against the SAS.

Not long before my meeting with the Phillips family, however, the first of my reservations was demolished when Baghdad suddenly granted permission to film after almost nine months of waiting. My encounter with Jeff, Steve and Veronica now convinced me that I had a genuine mission. My way had been opened, too, by other cracks that had recently begun to appear in the Bravo Two Zero story.

The previous December, in Auckland, New Zealand, Mike Coburn had fought and won a court case against UK Special Forces for the right to publish a third book about the mission, entitled *Soldier Five*. In his Statement of Defence, Coburn said that he wanted to set the record straight with regard to Vince Phillips, who, he declared, had been unfairly denigrated by Ryan in *The One That Got Away*, and made the scapegoat for much that went wrong. Elsewhere, Coburn wrote that Ryan had 'betrayed the ethos of the SAS, namely: honesty, integrity and loyalty, and defiled the names of those who died and are unable to defend themselves'. Under oath, Coburn and a fourth colleague, Mal, known in the story as 'Stan', stated that both Ryan and McNab had distorted the facts in their books. During the same court case, the former Chief of UK Special Forces, who had been CO of 22 SAS during the Gulf War, condemned McNab's book as 'untruthful' and referred to Ryan's 'selling out' of Vince as 'disgusting', despite the apparent revelations of the leaked

report. The most damning evidence of all, though, came from Peter Ratcliffe, former Regimental Sergeant Major of 22 SAS during the Gulf War who won the DCM for bravery and leadership while heading an SAS unit behind enemy lines. In his book *Eye of the Storm*, Ratcliffe wrote that neither McNab's nor Ryan's written accounts of the Bravo Two Zero mission tallied with the official debriefings they had given in the UK after the war. He likened both books to 'cheap war fiction' and stated for the record that in his opinion both Ryan and McNab had betrayed the proud traditions of the Regiment. He declared that though these authors hid behind pseudonyms, members of 22 SAS knew who they were and regarded them with 'contempt or ridicule or both'.

These new revelations not only suggested that the jury was out on both Ryan and McNab, but also that there were other mysteries attached to the Bravo Two Zero story. When I turned back to the books for a more detailed reading, I began to notice things I had missed first time around. In fact, apart from the basic outline of the story, they might in some places have been descriptions of different events. They did not even agree on what task the patrol had been set. While McNab stated that they had been sent to 'locate and destroy Scud missiles and landlines', ranging along a 250-kilometre stretch of road, Ryan maintained that their job was to mount a covert operation watching traffic movement. Many of the discrepancies were mutually exclusive – it didn't take a genius to realize that both accounts could not be correct. 'The public has been misled into believing they know the truth about Bravo Two Zero,' said Grant Illingworth, Coburn's lawyer in the Auckland trial, 'when the truth has been obscured and distorted.' Clearly there were many unresolved questions about Bravo Two Zero, quite apart from the reputation of

Vince Phillips, and I realized that my particular combination of experience – as an Arabic speaker, a desert explorer, and an ex-member of 23 SAS – well qualified me to investigate these discrepancies. Having seen the distress Ryan's account had caused the Phillips family, and in the light of the new evidence from Coburn, Ratcliffe and others, I promised Jeff, Steve and Veronica that I would visit Iraq, follow in the footsteps of the Bravo Two Zero patrol, and find out for myself what had happened. Above all, I would try to discover exactly how and where Vince had died.

# CHAPTER
# two

THANKS TO THE UN SANCTIONS there were no scheduled flights to Baghdad and we were obliged to drive in overland from Amman, Jordan, in cumbersome GMC vehicles provided by our fixers, Goran and Deilan: trim, energetic, quick-witted young Kurdish brothers who had worked for the BBC before shifting to escorting visiting film-crews. We left Amman on a hot day in May, and soon the built-up suburbs of the city fell away, to be replaced by the green, brown and red plains of the desert, a desolation stretching as far as the eye could see on both sides. Although this desert spans part of Syria, Jordan and Iraq, it is all of one piece geographically, and is properly referred to as the Badiyat Ash-Sham, or the Syrian Desert. Around 3000 BC, when the pyramids were being built in Egypt, the fringes of this desert were inhabited by a people called the Amorites, who had cattle, donkeys, sheep and goats. A thousand years later, having

acquired the camel, the Amorites were able to colonize the desert interior, and so the Badu – literally, the people of the Badiya, now known as the Bedouin – were born.

When most people think of deserts, they imagine sand dunes rolling on endlessly like the waves of a sea, but the Syrian Desert is nothing like that: in fact, there is very little sand. It is more like desolate, arid moorland, basically rocky or muddy, with stunted hills and high plateaux here and there, occasionally cut by steep-sided wadis. Although there are virtually no trees, the soil is fertile, raising sparse desert vegetation and often cultivated by the Bedouin after the rains.

On the way to the Iraq border we passed through Azraq, once a beautiful oasis of palm trees around a silver pool, and the site of the Roman castle that was T.E. Lawrence's base during his desert campaigns of 1917-18. The castle is still there, almost lost among streets of breeze-block housing, and a brief visit reminded me of the long experience the British had of fighting in this desert. Lawrence himself provided a comprehensive handbook on campaigning here, *Seven Pillars of Wisdom*, which outlines the extreme conditions to be experienced in this desert in winter. 'Nothing in Arabia could be more cutting that the north wind,' Lawrence wrote. 'It blew through our clothes as if we had none, fixed our fingers into claws.' Describing how he had to light fires under camels' bellies to revive them in the biting cold, Lawrence also said he sometimes had to drag his Bedouin soldiers up by their hair to prevent them from falling into the stupor that hypothermia brings. 'The winter's power drove leaders and men into the villages,' he wrote. 'Twice I ventured up to taste the snow-laden plateau . . . but life there was not tolerable. In the day it thawed a little, but at night it froze. The wind cut open the

skin: fingers lost power and sense of feel: cheeks shivered like dead leaves until they could shiver no more, then bound up muscles in a witless ache . . . ' Seventy years later, McNab echoed Lawrence, writing, 'I had known cold before, in the Arctic, but nothing like this. This was lying in a freezer cabinet feeling your body heat slowly slip away.'[3] Although McNab says that 1991 saw the coldest winter in the region in thirty years, winter temperatures in the western desert are commonly below freezing, and have been known to dip to an incredible minus 14 degrees Celsius. Bearing in mind that two of the patrol reportedly died of hypothermia, it seemed to me that Lawrence's experience might have proved a lesson worth learning.

Although David Stirling is credited with founding the SAS, the principles on which the Regiment operates were developed by Lawrence during the Arab campaign in 1916–17 against the Ottoman Turks. The Turks' lifeline in Arabia was the Hejaz railway, completed in 1908, which connected their garrisons there with the outside world. But the railway ran through 800 miles of desert in which the Bedouin could come and go as they pleased. Lawrence saw that the way to victory for irregular fighters was not to confront superior forces, but to hit the enemy with a small, mobile force at its weakest points – bridges, locomotives, watering-stations – and run away into the desert where the Turks could not follow. He had discovered desert power. It was this strategy that David Stirling took up when he formed L Detachment of the Special Air Service Brigade in North Africa in 1941. When his original idea of dropping trained saboteurs by parachute failed, however, he turned to the real desert experts, the Long Range Desert Group (LRDG), who had perfected the techniques of desert motoring and navigation. With the LRDG as their transport and navigation arm, SAS patrols were able to hit enemy

airfields and supply dumps and disappear back into the desert, just as Lawrence had done on his camels. The raiding partnership between the LRDG and the SAS was brilliantly successful, and accounted for more German aircraft on the ground than the RAF did in the air. The key to desert power, whether by camel or car, was mobility. As the CO of the LRDG, Guy Prenderghast, told Stirling after his first abortive parachute drop, 'Once actually on the ground, a party of men moving about on foot in the desert cannot get far.' The SAS is proud of its history and traditions, yet some of the very principles on which it had been founded seem to have been forgotten in the Bravo Two Zero affair.

THE OFFICIALS AT THE IRAQI border were gruff, but no gruffer than such men are almost everywhere, and the formalities took up no more than an hour and a half. The only bug-bear was the compulsory AIDS test, which none of us had particularly been looking forward to, but for which we had prepared by bringing our own sterile needles. As it happened, we didn't need them. A judicious handshake from our 22-year-old Kurdish fixer, Goran, seemed to have settled the matter. Once through the frontier checkpoints, it was as if a prison door had slammed shut behind us, and it was difficult to rid myself of the idea that we were entering enemy territory. Perhaps it was the succession of giant portraits of a stern-looking Saddam Hussein that set my mind on edge, but it was an effort to forget that some dark things had happened in this country not so long ago. No doubt they were still happening. Goran told me that the Iraqi national football team had recently lost a match against Turkestan. Uday, the President's son, and Chairman of the team, had had his players

tortured to make sure they never lost again. The story made me laugh, until I remembered that there was no British Embassy in Baghdad to run to if things went wrong. From now on we were on our own.

The light was already dwindling as we sped away from the border along a superbly built multi-lane highway with virtually no other traffic on it, taking us straight into the heart of Iraq. The highway had been constructed by a German company and had been completed, but not opened, by the time the Gulf War broke out. In January 1991 it had proved a major obstacle to a motorized SAS patrol – commanded by RSM Peter Ratcliffe – which had needed to cross it in order to reach the target, a missile command and control station nicknamed Victor Two. The desert here was punctuated by the black tents of Bedouin, who, but for the motor vehicles parked outside, appeared to be living much the same lives as their Amorite ancestors had four thousand years ago. As darkness descended across the desert I fell asleep in the passenger seat, and when I woke again we were in Baghdad.

Having seen the surreal, shell-shocked streets of west Beirut in the early '90s, I had been expecting something similar in Baghdad. In fact it was a bustling, pleasant, modern city on the banks of the Tigris, with well-stocked shops and packed restaurants, showing few scars of the Allied bombing of recent years. There was nothing more out of the ordinary, indeed, than the occasional S60 anti-aircraft battery on the high buildings. There was no heavy military or police presence on the streets, and we were allowed to come and go without restrictions, wandering across the Tigris bridges – all rebuilt since 1991 – and through the flea-market and Ottoman bazaars. The first thing that struck me about the Iraqis was their extreme

friendliness and courtesy. I'd been prepared by the western media for fanatics capable of lynching a foreigner at the drop of a hat. Instead, I found open, ordinary, civilized folk getting on with their lives as best they could, without any apparent animosity towards me at all. Twice I entered an old teashop in the centre of Baghdad – a place of crude wooden benches, with a bank of gas-jets heating water in battered brass vessels, where men sat chatting quietly or nodding over hookah-pipes. Several men came over to ask me where I was from, and when I told them, they questioned me without the slightest hint of malice.

There was little obvious poverty in the main streets, but UN officials had recently reported an alarming rise in infant mortality, and unemployment in Baghdad was reckoned to be at fifty per cent. The souqs were full of valuable items that were going for a song – gold watches, cameras, Dunhill cigarette-lighters – no doubt ditched by their owners in a desperate last attempt to get some capital. It was as if the contents of everyone's attics had suddenly hit the market at rock-bottom prices. For six dollars I bought a British-made prismatic compass in perfect condition, which in London would have cost me three hundred dollars.

The features I encountered most frequently were the ubiquitous portraits of Saddam Hussein, which glared or smiled down from every street corner. These portraits represented the President in various guises: the paternal Saddam cuddling a child, the military Saddam in bemedalled uniform, the Arab prince in stately robes, the Iraqi Fellah in knotted headcloth, the sociable Saddam squatting with a glass of tea, the devout Saddam performing his prayers, and the westernized, modern Saddam resplendent in a white suit – there was even a relaxed Saddam talking on the telephone. There was

something for almost everyone here – a man for all seasons, I thought. The real Saddam, however, appeared to be keeping a low profile, and sometimes I began to wonder if he actually existed at all.

Uday was the number two or three at the Ministry of Information, a grave-looking man who had been a professional journalist in Paris before the war, and who had the rather disconcerting habit of addressing me as 'my dear'. In his spacious but spartan office on the top floor of the Ministry building he welcomed us with a prepared speech about the resilient nature of the Iraqi people and how you could not defeat a nation with a civilization going back six thousand years. It was propaganda, but I took his point. The earliest civilizations known to man – Babylon, Sumer, Akkad, Assyria and others – had flourished in the valleys of the Euphrates and the Tigris thousands of years before Christ. Beside them, even the ancient Egyptians were newcomers, and the British and Americans little more than literate barbarians. When I went over what I had come here to do, and emphasized that I wanted to follow the routes of the Bravo Two Zero patrol on foot, he shook his head and looked worried. 'That is difficult,' he said. 'Very difficult indeed.' I assumed he had thought it would be enough for me to pursue my research in Baghdad. When I continued, saying that I hoped to find eyewitnesses – the shepherd-boy Ryan and McNab said had spotted them, the driver of the bulldozer who had approached their LUP, local militia involved in the initial firefight, the driver of the taxi they had hijacked, witnesses of the battles the patrol had fought near the Syrian border, the men who found Vince Phillips's body, personnel who had interrogated the patrol – he actually laughed. 'I have read your CV, my dear,' he said. 'You should know very well that people such as this shepherd-boy are nomads. They move on

all the time. It is very unlikely that they will be in the same place now, and how will you find them? As for the military personnel involved, we are talking about ten years ago, when we had a huge conscript army. Since then people have died and moved all round the country, records have been lost or burned or blown up, and the whole system of administration has been changed. How will you find a taxi driver when you don't know the man's name or even the number of his car? There are thousands of taxi drivers in Iraq. You are looking for needles in haystacks – it is most unlikely that you will find any eyewitnesses. Why don't you stay in Baghdad, shoot some film here instead?'

I left his office feeling depressed. Nobody in the Ministry of Information seemed to have heard of the SAS or Bravo Two Zero. In the scale of a war in which at least 100,000 Iraqis died and 63,000 were captured, I realized suddenly, an eight-man patrol was very small fry indeed. And yet McNab wrote that the patrol had accounted for at least two hundred and fifty Iraqi casualties, so someone, somewhere, must have felt the impact of the operation.

For the next few days I hung around the hotel disconsolately waiting for news, and it began to occur to me that the Iraqis had no intention of letting me wander around their deserts. The government had applied for the UN sanctions to be lifted again and in some quarters opinion was shifting in their favour. Probably, I reflected gloomily, they had seen an opportunity to get a British film-crew into Baghdad and score some sympathetic foreign coverage free of charge.

My mood wasn't heightened when Ahmad, a stringy, reserved and rather morose man from the Ministry of Information, suggested a visit to the Amiriya Bunker to pass the time. It was a civic air-raid

shelter situated in a residential area of Baghdad that had been hit by American missiles in February 1991, and four hundred civilians – among them many children – had been killed. It was a sobering experience, to say the least. The place had been left almost exactly as it was when it had been hit, with a vast hole punched through a roof of stressed concrete ten feet thick. The walls and floor were still blackened from the blast, and Ahmad told me that the rescue services hadn't been able to open the vast steel doors, so by the time they had cut through them with oxyacetylene torches, most of the survivors had been burned to ashes. Actually, the bunker had been hit by two laser-guided missiles: an incendiary rocket that had come through the air-vent and the explosive missile which had caused the gaping wound in the roof. Photos of the dead children decorated the walls, as well as pictures of the scorched and mutilated bodies being removed. The Coalition had claimed that the bunker was being used by Saddam Hussein's military command, and even that the apparent civilian casualties had been 'invented' by the Iraqis. However, foreign reporters who were allowed to inspect the place at the time found no evidence that it had been used by the military, and Alan Little of the BBC, who watched the mangled bodies being carried out, concluded that this was something totally beyond the ability of the Iraqi Ministry of Information to stage-manage. 'This morning we saw the charred and mutilated remains of those nearest the door,' he told viewers. 'They were piled into the back of a truck: many were barely recognizable as human. Men from the district pushed and jostled through the crowd to find news of their families, many distressed to the point of panic.'

Whatever the case, Amiriya was a salutary reminder that modern war is not an affair of lone warriors, but of billions of dollars-

worth of technology, and its end result is too often places like this. I tried to imagine what it must have been like for those trapped in here when the missile struck, and turned away with a shudder.

The only high point of those days of waiting was when Ahmad insinuated himself into the lobby of my hotel one morning clutching a newspaper article in Arabic. The piece, dating from earlier in the year, was an interview with a man called Adnan Badawi, who had been a passenger in a taxi that had been hijacked by a group of 'British commandos' near Krabilah in western Iraq, on 26 January 1991. The article excited me – it was the first independent evidence from an Iraqi source that the Bravo Two Zero mission had actually happened. Moreover, the article included not only Adnan's name, but that of the taxi driver and – even better – the registration number of the taxi itself. The first needle in the haystack had at least been glimpsed, if not found, and Ahmad told me that he was taking steps to contact Adnan, who lived in Mosul in the far north of Iraq. The bad news was that further permission from the Ministry of Defence was required before I could visit the Anbar region of western Iraq, where the action had taken place. But in any case, he concluded, I should probably be able to start on Wednesday.

Wednesday came, but permission did not. Ahmad told me the expedition was rescheduled for Saturday. I had already been hanging around for more than a week and my time was slipping away. It was May, and incredibly hot in Baghdad, and if I waited any longer it would be high summer, and almost suicidal to travel on foot in the desert. I asked Ahmad for a meeting with Uday, was granted one, and went up to see him with my associate producer, Nigel Morris. 'Look, Mr Uday,' I said, as politely and firmly as I could. 'We were given visas on the basis of this project – the Bravo Two Zero story

– and I sent you a full outline before we came. I understood we had permission to do it already. We have been completely open about what we intended to do from the beginning and there is no secret about it. If it is not the case that we were given permission, then please tell us now. Our time is running out and I have to say that unless we really do leave on Saturday we shall have to return to the UK.'

Uday's face turned black and I waited for the axe to fall. I knew I was sticking my neck out; I thought of the footballers the President's son had had tortured for losing against Turkestan. 'You have to realize this country is still at war, my dear,' he said, dryly. 'We are suffering under UN sanctions and things can't be organized just like that. It is the military who are dragging their feet, not the Ministry of Information. The problem is that you cannot go into that area without a representative from the military, and nobody is going to walk in the desert at this time of year.'

I smiled. 'That's no problem,' I said. 'The representative can travel in our GMC vehicles with the film-crew while I walk.'

'Yes,' he said. 'But then how are they going to be able to see what you get up to?'

'I can rendezvous with the vehicles every few hours.'

Uday considered this and said he would see what he could do. He picked up the telephone. By the time I had reached the door, he was bellowing into the receiver like a bull.

# CHAPTER
# three

WE LEFT ON SATURDAY AS scheduled, heading north towards the Anbar region in a convoy of four GMCs with five film-crew and four drivers. There were also two minders: Ali from the Ministry of Information and Abu Omar from the Ministry of Defence. The minders were so different in personality and approach that I sometimes wondered if they were deliberately working the 'good cop, bad cop' routine. Ali, the civilian, was tall, moon-faced, pot-bellied and dishevelled-looking, an exuberant, talkative extrovert who spoke no English but was for ever slapping people on the back and roaring out their names. Abu Omar, the military man, was small and dapper with immaculately pressed suits and carefully combed and oiled hair. He was aloof and disdainful, taciturn to the point of rudeness, and gave the impression that the last thing in the world he needed was to accompany a bunch of Englishmen into the desert. We drove up the

Euphrates Valley, through smoky industrial towns and villages huddling in palm groves, and halted at the area headquarters at Rumadi to meet our military escort: a detachment of six soldiers under a lieutenant, in an ordinary Toyota pick-up with a machine-gun mounted on the back. When I quizzed Ali about the escort, he told me it was for our protection. 'The place is full of wolves and bandits,' he said.

Ali had served in an infantry battalion during the Iran-Iraq war, and shivered when I asked him about it. 'It was terrible,' he said. 'It was hand-to-hand fighting, up close so you could see the enemy, butchering them with knives and bayonets, and them butchering us. May God protect us from the devil, I never again want to see anything like that!'

The Iran-Iraq war lasted eight years, but did not resolve any of the issues over which it had been fought. Saddam Hussein's original excuse for his 1980 invasion of western Iran was to end the Iranian monopoly of the Shatt al-Arab waterway, conceded to her in a treaty of 1975. The war consisted mainly of bloody World War I-style offensives against immovable tiers of trenches, in which the attackers were frequently mown down like sheep. Both sides used chemical weapons, and in 1985 both began lobbing missiles against each other's capitals. In 1987 Iran made the fatal mistake of targeting Kuwaiti tankers in the Gulf, bring down upon her the wrath of the USA, which had hitherto been covertly supplying her with weapons. Reviled by world opinion, and finding it increasingly difficult to buy arms, Iran was obliged to negotiate a peace treaty in 1988. Saddam Hussein crowed over the masses of Iranian armour and artillery his armies had captured, but it was a Pyrrhic victory: up to 1.7 million people had perished in the war, but not an inch of ground had been gained.

In 1990, Kuwait, a tiny but oil-rich desert princedom on Iraq's

southern border, pressed Saddam Hussein for repayment of certain loans she had made to her neighbour during the war. In reply, Saddam accused the Kuwaitis of contravening the OPEC agreement by overproducing oil, costing Iraq fourteen million dollars in lost revenues. He also claimed that Kuwait had been pumping crude oil from the Ramailah oilfield, whose ownership was disputed and, throwing in Iraq's traditional claim on Kuwaiti territory for good measure, invaded the princedom with one hundred thousand troops and twelve hundred tanks. It was 2 August 1990.

The UN Security Council promptly denounced the invasion, declaring a trade embargo against Iraq, and by 14 August the spearhead brigade of the US 82nd Airborne Division had arrived in Saudi Arabia to secure the country's oil-reserves. The first phase of the Coalition operation – Desert Shield – was a protective action designed to block an Iraqi invasion of Saudi Arabia, and to gain time for a massive concentration of men and matériel from thirty-two countries, including Britain, France, Italy, Egypt, Syria, Qatar, Oman, the UAE and Bahrain, as well as Saudi Arabia and the USA. The build-up of Iraqi forces continued, however, and by November the Coalition was facing no less than twenty-six divisions in the Kuwait theatre, comprising more than 450,000 men. It was becoming clear to Allied Commander-in-Chief H. Norman Schwarzkopf and his political bosses that nothing short of a counter-offensive would oust the Iraqis from Kuwait, and by mid-November he had finalized his plan of attack. On 29 November the UN Security Council lit the fuse of war by authorizing the use of force if the Iraqis did not pull out of Kuwait by 15 January 1991.

General Schwarzkopf, nicknamed 'The Bear', had devised a two-phase offensive against the Iraqis, designated Desert Storm.

First, wave after wave of Allied bombers would go in, hitting strategic targets, cutting the command infrastructure and gaining control of the skies. When this had been achieved, the Air Force would turn its attention to the Iraqi army, pounding their artillery, armour and static defences mercilessly until the morale of Saddam Hussein's troops had been comprehensively worn down. Only then would the massed divisions of the Coalition ground forces go in for the kill.

Within days of the invasion of Kuwait, the two available squadrons of 22 SAS, G and D, were put on standby in Hereford, and while the SAS Intelligence Unit began a frantic round of briefings and reports, G Squadron was despatched to the United Arab Emirates to begin refresher training in desert warfare. B Squadron – to which McNab and Ryan belonged – was currently holding down the Regiment's Special Projects or counter-revolutionary warfare role, and A Squadron was in Columbia, training teams to fight the drug barons, but each was duly scheduled to desert retraining in turn.

For the first five months of the war, the SAS had no designated role: the US 5th Special Forces Group and US Marine Corps were handling reconnaissance on the Kuwaiti frontier, and the only suitable job for the SAS that was vacant was the rescue of hostages. There were more than sixteen hundred British citizens in Iraqi custody in Iraq and Kuwait, so freeing them would hardly be an easy business. Indeed, a British team tasked with planning a hostage-recovery operation calculated that it would require a force of at least Brigade strength – more than three times the manpower of all three SAS Regiments combined – and would still probably result in more casualties than the number of hostages released. The plan was scrapped in December, when Saddam Hussein released the hostages anyway.

A, B, and D Squadrons were all deployed in the Gulf by 2 January, but they still had no official role in the General's concept of Desert Storm. To Schwarzkopf, who had seen the bungling of US Special Forces in Vietnam and Grenada, this was to be an air and missile operation, backed up by heavy armoured and mechanized infantry units. What the hell could Special Forces do, he demanded, that a Stealth fighter could not?

In the second week of December, the Commander of British forces in the Gulf, General Sir Peter de la Billière – a former CO of 22 SAS – had given the Regiment instructions to start devising plans for deep-penetration raids behind Iraqi lines, saying that they should be ready to go by 15 January. It was only shortly before this deadline that de la Billière managed finally to win Schwarzkopf over, with a formal presentation involving detailed maps and graphics. The SAS task, he explained, would be to 'cut roads and create diversions which would draw Iraqi forces away from the main front and sow fears in the mind of the enemy that some major operation was brewing on his right flank'.[4] The presentation might have convinced Schwarzkopf, but to the Regiment's rank and file it did not disguise the fact that there was still nothing specific for the SAS to do. It was certainly the concept upon which SAS founder David Stirling had based the original Regiment back in 1941, but since the regular unit had been reconstituted for the Malayan Emergency in 1949, it had generally used its skills for more strategic roles. But it was better than nothing: the SAS Regiment is a very expensive outfit to keep up, and despite de la Billière's decree that he would not send in the SAS in unless there was a proper job for them, this was the biggest deployment of troops since World War II and the Regiment had to be seen to earn its pay.

Not since 1945 had such a large contingent of British Special Forces been assembled in one place. The SAS group had been reorganized after the Falklands War into UK Special Forces, commanded by a brigadier, and including 21 SAS, 22 SAS and 23 SAS, as well as the Royal Marines Special Boat Service (SBS), and 63 and 264 SAS Signals Squadrons. The three SAS regular 'sabre' or operational squadrons deployed in the Gulf were supported by fifteen men of R Squadron, the little-publicized territorial unit whose members are trained to provide individual replacements for the regular squadrons in time of need. This brought the operational strength of the SAS to about three hundred men, though with special forces aircrews from the RAF, supporting arms and an SBS Squadron, the UKSF contingent numbered almost double that.

At 0247 hours on 17 January 1991, General Schwarzkopf received word that the first targets of Desert Storm – two Iraqi early-warning radar installations on the Saudi Arabian border – had been taken out. A dozen Apache helicopters of the 101st Airborne streaked in only ten metres above the desert floor and hit them from five kilometres away with deadly laser-guided Hellfire missiles. The Apache flight had been followed up by eight F-15 fighters tasked to skewer the nearest Iraqi air-defence command centre, opening up a brace of blind corridors through which thousands of Coalition jets would swarm to hit 240 strategic targets all over Iraq.

While the Allied airstrikes continued, the SAS was transferring on C130 transport planes from its HQ in the United Arab Emirates and forming up at its FOB (Forward Operating Base) at al-Jauf in Saudi Arabia, a day's drive south of the Iraqi frontier. Equipped with Land Rover 110s fitted with Browning machine-guns, GPMGs (general purpose machine-guns) and Milan missiles, A and D Squadrons were

preparing to launch their deep-penetration raids, but wondering if there was really any place for them in the midst of this hi-tech circus. 'The air war already seemed to be going the way Schwarzkopf had predicted,' Peter Ratcliffe wrote. 'Who needed Special Forces?'[5]

On 18 January the situation changed dramatically for the SAS. At 0300 hours that morning Iraq fired seven Scud missiles at Israel, to be followed later by another three. Israeli casualties were, luckily, slight, but Israeli Premier Yitshak Shamir came up fighting, and demanded the right to retaliate with a hundred aircraft and a commando attack, flying across Saudi Arabian airspace. Schwarzkopf's nightmare scenario was about to unfold right before his eyes. If the Israelis were to hit Iraq, the Coalition the Americans had worked so hard to build would be badly strained, or even shattered.

'The Bear' had discounted the antiquated Scud as a tactical weapon, but had to concede that as a political threat it was ideal. The Coalition must be protected at any price, and the price was a diversion from its 'real' job of thirty per cent of Allied air power to execute what became known as the 'Great Scud Hunt'.

Schwarzkopf was right in believing that the Scud was outdated. Based loosely on the German V2 of WW2 notoriety, these ballistic missiles had been produced in Russia in the 1950s and had been imported by the Iraqis in the 70s and 80s during the Iran-Iraq war. Flying about 30 kilometres above the earth, at a speed of 5000 km an hour, the Scud did not possess sufficient range for the Iraqis to hit Tehran, while Baghdad was vulnerable to attack by Iranian missiles because it stood nearer the border. Consequently the Iraqis cannibalized their existing Scuds, extending their length and fuel capacity, but reducing the power of the warheads. The ploy was successful, and in 1988 Scud attacks on Tehran accounted for some 8000

casualties. Saddam Hussein was now intending to bring Israel into the war by launching similar attacks on Tel Aviv.

Though President Bush assured Shamir that evening that all known fixed Scud bases had been blitzed by Coalition sorties, most of the Israel-bound Scuds had been fired from mobile transporter-erector launchers in western Iraq. Allied fighters could make mince-meat of these vehicles – if they could be located, and locating them was the problem. It was often beyond the scope of even the most sophisticated surveillance equipment when the TELs were hidden in bunkers, or even under a convenient motorway bridge. Though Bush eventually persuaded Shamir to desist, at least temporarily, it was clear that the mobile launchers had to be found. Here at last was a job that the Mk 1 human eyeball could do better than any machine – a job custom-built for the SAS, and one that the astute de la Billière had considered a possibility from the beginning. On 20 January, 128 men of A and D Squadrons, already crossing the Iraqi border in search of opportunity targets, received official sanction from Schwarzkopf to hunt the Scuds.

Only half of B Squadron had been deployed at al-Jauf, the others having been left in the United Arab Emirates on security detail, and that half – including McNab, Ryan and Phillips – was divided into three teams, Bravo One Zero, Bravo Two Zero and Bravo One Niner, which would be flown in by Chinook to three specified MSRs (Main Supply Routes) deep behind enemy lines. Bravo Two Zero consisted of eight men. The patrol commander, 'McNab', was a Londoner, the son of a Greek nightclub owner and his English mistress, who had been brought up by foster parents and had decided to join the army to escape a life of petty theft and delinquency. Now a sergeant, with eight or nine years' service in the SAS, his main

combat experience had been in Northern Ireland with the Royal Green Jackets – his parent unit – where he had shot and wounded one terrorist and killed another. Married, with one child from a previous marriage, McNab was a fast-talking, articulate Jack-the-lad who considered that every professional soldier deserved at least one proper war, and this was his. His second-in-command, Sgt Vince Phillips, was older than the rest of the team – at 36 he had only a couple more years to serve. Phillips was the odd-man-out in Bravo Two Zero because, unlike the others, he belonged to A Squadron and had been posted in to fill a gap at the last moment. 'Ryan', a corporal, was a Geordie from the Tyneside region, a highly intelligent and determined man who had served in 23 SAS (V) before joining 22 SAS. Married, with one child, Ryan was the most experienced patrol medic in the team. 'Dinger' – a prodigious smoker and drinker – was a lance-corporal who had served in the Parachute Regiment prior to the SAS, as had his comrade, Trooper Steven 'Legs' Lane, a relative newcomer to the Regiment, who was married with two children and who held the vital job of patrol signaller. Robert 'Bob' Consiglio was a small but powerful man of Anglo-Italian descent who had resigned from the Royal Marines to take SAS selection and had passed first time. The remaining two members of Bravo Two Zero were both Antipodeans. 'Stan' – the only university graduate in the patrol – had served in the Rhodesian army, but had emigrated to Australia, where he had trained as a dentist. He had given it all up to move to Britain and join the SAS. Finally there was Mike Coburn, 'Mark', a New Zealander who had originally served in the Australian SAS. All eight men were highly trained professional soldiers, the best of the best Special Forces unit in the world.

On the evening of 22 January 1991, Bravo Two Zero was flown

to a point about 187 miles north of the border, within striking distance of the most northerly of the three MSRs. Touching down at
around 2000 hours that night, they lay in the cold desert in all-round
defence until the Chinook had disappeared, then picked up their
massive burdens – 95 kilos, about 209 pounds of equipment each –
and began to lug it towards an LUP (lying up point) they had chosen somewhere near a kink in the road. To find that LUP – the first
identifiable point in the Bravo Two Zero story – was my own objective when I arrived in Anbar, a little more than ten years on.

# CHAPTER
## four

FROM STANFORD'S IN THE Haymarket, I had obtained a
1:500,000 air chart of Iraq. It was similar to the ones Bravo Two
Zero had been issued with, but of a smaller scale – theirs was the
1:250,000 scale version, which was not available to the public. Luckily, though, in *The One That Got Away* Ryan had reproduced a section of his own map with Bravo Two Zero's routes marked on it,
and McNab had supplied a sketch-map drawn to scale at the end of
his book. By painstaking protractor work I had been able to trans-
fer the routes to my own larger-scale map with some accuracy. The
patrol's lying up point – their 'first base' – had been in sight of a main
road, so assuming McNab and Ryan had put it in the right place, it
would be relatively easy to find by simply driving out along that road
a measured number of kilometres from the nearest town, al-
Haqlaniya.

Just before we reached al-Haqlaniya, Ali, in the lead vehicle, turned off sharply down a road to the right. Wondering what on earth he was doing, I had my driver overtake and flagged him down. 'Where are you going?' I demanded.

He announced majestically that there were some Bedouin living in this direction whom he thought might know something about what happened in the Gulf War. A red light started blinking in my head; I knew this tendency had to be nipped in the bud. If the minders intended to guide me and show me where I had to go, then the story would immediately lose its credibility. I had no intention whatsoever of playing pawn to Iraqi propaganda – I had to be certain that any-thing I discovered was absolutely independent. I stopped the convoy and called everyone over to me. 'Now listen,' I told them in Arabic. 'I have come here to do a job, and I know what I'm doing. I know where I am going and to whom I want to talk. I speak Arabic and I am famil-iar with deserts, and if there are places to be found and witnesses to be talked to, I will find them myself, or I won't find them at all. I am sure you know your jobs, but on no account must you interfere with mine. We must do it my way, and go where I want to go, even if I am wrong. As I understand it, you are here only to make sure I don't enter a restricted area or film forbidden items, not to tell me where I should go. I don't want to be told to go here and talk to some-one there, and unless that is understood, we can go back to Baghdad right now.'

I had said it rather too pugnaciously, and for moment there was a strained silence. Then Ali grinned nervously and said he had worked with news film-crews before and knew what was required. He had only been trying to help. Abu Omar sneered and turned away, but neither of the minders ever tried to interfere directly again.

We turned back to our original route and, bypassing al-Haqlaniya, moved south of west along the road that led to the pumping-stations H1, H2 and H3, and eventually to Jordan, running parallel with the great watercourse known as the Wadi Hawran. To our north was a line of electricity pylons which angled sharply away across stony, flat desert after a few kilometres. I was following our progress on my Magellan – a hand-held global positioning system unit (GPS) the size of a mobile telephone, which gave my latitude and longitude within a few metres. It was a slightly more sophisticated version of the GPS unit the Bravo Two Zero patrol had carried with them on the operation itself. Now, I experienced a sudden burst of excitement. This was definitely it, I thought, the Main Supply Route that had been Bravo Two Zero's objective on the night of 22 January 1991. As we sped along, I found myself wondering what McNab's patrol had really been doing here in the first place.

In his book, McNab relates that the Officer Commanding B Squadron specifically tasked his patrol with locating and cutting communications landlines, and locating and destroying Scuds. The duration of the operation was to be fourteen days, and the patrol was to range 250 kilometres along this very road, seeking out and bumping opportunity targets – an active and aggressive role. But though McNab devotes several pages to describing how the patrol intended to knock out the Scuds, Ryan's description of the OC's briefing is entirely different. He quotes the same officer as telling the patrol that their job was to gather intelligence – to find a lying up point, set up an observation post on the road and report back to the forward operating base (FOB) on enemy traffic movement, especially Scuds. In Ryan's account the task is essentially passive. He maintains that the patrol would remain hidden, manning the OP for

ten days, after which it would be relocated by air. He mentions nothing about 'destroying Scuds', or patrolling 250 kilometres along the MSR, but does state that a subsidiary task was to blow up any fibre optic cables the patrol might happen to find while going about their principal task. Though McNab's version is the more dashing and romantic, the road-watch OP is classic SAS procedure, with a history going back to the Long Range Desert Group. In 1942, LRDG patrols set up OPs along the Via Balbia – the main German supply route along the coast of North Africa – to watch and report enemy movements in order to verify the decrypts British Intelligence had obtained through cracking the Enigma code. They had succeeded brilliantly, hiding their vehicles behind dunes or in wadis, rotating two men out each night to man the OP, which was often little more than a rock or a clump of grass. Later, throughout the Cold War, it was the main task of 21 and 23 SAS, the territorial units, to dig and operate similar OPs in Europe – a fact that Ryan knew well, having originally served in 23 SAS. Of the three road-watch patrols sent out from B Squadron, two elected to go on foot. Why send foot patrols to knock out highly mobile and heavily protected Scud launchers, I wondered? A mobile patrol could do the job far more efficiently with its Milan missiles, and as Schwarzkopf had rightly said, a Stealth fighter could do it even better. Even the A and D Squadron patrols that had gone out on 20 January had been directed to locate rather than destroy Scuds, transmitting their locations to the Air Arm so that they could be taken out with ease. Expecting a foot patrol to destroy Scud erector-launchers with the whole of the desert to hide in seemed to defy military logic, while going in on foot if you intended to lie hidden in one place for ten days and be relocated by aircraft at least made some kind of sense. Ryan states clearly that if the patrol

sighted a Scud convoy on the road, their task was not to attack it, but to relay the information back to base by both satcom and patrol radio, upon receipt of which an aircraft would be vectored in to take the missile out [6]. That the patrol planned to put in a hide is also indicated by the tremendous weights they were hefting, which Ryan puts even heavier than McNab, at 120 kilos per man. Although McNab emphasizes the large amount of ordnance they had with them – plastic explosive, Claymore and Elsie anti-personnel mines, timers, detonators, primers and detonating cord – the patrol was also carrying hundreds of fibre sandbags, camouflage nets and full-sized shovels, the function of which can only have been to put in an OP. Though Ryan states that they intended to dig into the bank of a wadi, McNab maintains that the shovels were for digging up fibre optic cables.

The road climbed a low escarpment, passed buildings and plantations and descended through a series of bends into a valley, with a fifteen-foot ridge of crumbling basalt to our right and, to our left, the bronze-green folds, furrows and ripples of the desert. I stopped the car and looked around. According to my best assessment from the map and the Magellan, we were now within a few hundred metres of Bravo Two Zero's LUP. I jumped out and looked around. To the south, the rocky table-land fell away suddenly about 250 metres from the road into a system of deep-sided wadis, and as I climbed down to investigate the various re-entrants I wondered if the LUP would be recognizable: both Ryan and McNab had described a sort of cave or overhang, divided in the middle by a detached, wedge-shaped rock.

One re-entrant I followed ended in a narrow cleft wide enough only to hold a single man; this could not be the place in which eight

SAS men had holed up. A second branch-wadi terminated in a bowl-shaped depression, with signs of erosion and tiny caves cut into the rock walls. I looked at McNab's and Ryan's descriptions again – Ryan's in particular was very specific, recording that the overhang went back well under the wadi wall, and that the detached rock stood about seven feet high. I was certain this couldn't be it – the caves were no more than eroded apertures, too small to have hidden even a dog. I was beginning to think that either I had made an error in my map-reading or there had been no LUP here at all when I stumbled on a cul-de-sac at the end of a third branch-wadi. I stared at it, amazed at what I had found. The space was perhaps ten metres wide and filled with vegetation and stones. On the eastern side was a deep rock overhang, like a shelter, enclosing a pocket of shade. There was a smaller overhang to the right, divided from the larger one by a vast, detached boulder, almost pyramid-shaped, behind which a group of men huddling together might have been completely hidden. I went over the descriptions yet again and knew there could be no possible doubt. I was standing on one of the sacred sites of late twentieth century Special Operations. I had found Bravo Two Zero's LUP.

As cover from view, the wadi-end was perfect, but as a defensive position, as McNab himself says, it left much to be desired. I searched the place thoroughly, thrilled by the knowledge that I was almost certainly the first Westerner to visit this spot since Bravo Two Zero had holed up here in January 1991. This had been the place where the patrol had been compromised and where Vince Phillips had spent his last peaceful night. My search revealed nothing but the rim of a canvas bucket, tucked between some stones, but I pulled at it gingerly, knowing there could still be booby-traps here, even ten years later. Luckily, there was no flash-bang, and when I examined it

I couldn't be certain whether it was British army issue or some Bedouin thing. Letting it go, I scrambled out of the wadi on the northern side, trying to match my view against what McNab and Ryan might have seen as the day dawned on the morning of 23 January 1991, ten years before.

Although McNab's MSR could not be seen from here because of the dead ground, I knew it was there, no more than a stone's throw away, because our convoy of four orange and white GMCs was parked up there, on my side of the granite ridge that cut across the desert to the north. Due east lay a rambling clutch of what appeared to be farm-buildings and a water-tower among sparse bushes and shrubs, standing on a flat-topped hill. Curiously, McNab does mention seeing a house with trees and a water-tower, but due south of this position rather than east, where I could see none. Even more curiously, he cites an almost identical settlement – trees, water-tower, a building – as having stood due east of the point where the patrol had been dropped by helicopter, which, according to him, lay twenty kilometres south of here. Ryan does not report having seen the farm at all, but recalls having heard dogs barking within five hundred metres of the helicopter drop-off point, which he says was only two kilometres south of the place I was standing. If I had come here expecting to get a clear picture of what had really happened, I was disappointed. The only thing I could be sure of was that I had found the LUP.

# CHAPTER
# five

THE MORE I LOOKED AT THE farm-house, the nearer it appeared. I could have sworn it was less than a kilometre away. Of course, it might not have been there at all ten years ago, but even so, it was still possible that someone there might at least be able to give me hearsay information, or even put me in touch with a witness. I decided to go up to the house, pacing out my way with the Magellan as I did so. The ground was flattish and stony, interspersed with patches of baked clay, but there was another plunging wadi between me and the house which had signs of cultivation in its bed. As I slithered down the slope into it, dogs began to bark. I came up into a dusty driveway set among withered stone-pine, eucalyptus and mesquite trees that were obviously having a hard time coping with moisture loss. The house was exactly six hundred metres from the lying up point, and close up it was huge and spartan, with concrete pillars supporting a

wide verandah that ran the whole length of its façade. In the shade of the verandah stood a huge earthenware pot full of water, and on the wall was what looked like the stuffed head of a wolf. There were other outbuildings hidden behind it that I could not see properly, but the water storage tank I had noticed from the wadi was obviously an antique – rusted to pieces and full of holes. A veiled woman in loose brown robes was working around the corner of the verandah, and when I called out to her, 'As-salaam alaykum – Peace be on you,' she returned my greeting and invited me to come into the shade and sit down. Soon children of every age, dressed in dishdashas and shamaghs, were buzzing around me like flies. Carpets were rolled out on the verandah and cushions brought, and soon I was being offered cool water from the earthenware pot and, very shortly, glasses of sweet tea.

The reception was familiar to me and although I was a complete stranger here I felt at home. I knew instinctively that these people were Bedouin – there were a thousand tell-tale signs: their graciousness, the way they dressed and moved, their spontaneous welcome to a guest. Bedouin customs are universal all over the Middle East and North Africa, and one of the most sacred is hospitality. Their code holds that anyone is welcome in a Bedouin home for three days, and in that time the host is duty-bound to give him the best of what he has to eat and drink, and to protect him from harm, even against his own family. This code holds even if the guest is an enemy with whom the family has a blood feud, and in that case, even when the guest has left, the host and his family cannot pursue him until the bread and salt he has eaten in the house is reckoned to have passed out of his system. One of the worst insults that can be lodged against a Bedouin is that he 'did not know a guest', and since the

Bedouin live by the cult of reputation rather than possessions, families and individuals actually compete with one another to gain renown for open-handedness.

Eventually a rugged-looking young man with curly hair and a blue stubble appeared and shook hands. He looked about twenty years old, and wore a dirty white dishdasha with no headcloth. We exchanged greetings and he sat down next to me self-consciously. No Bedouin will ask directly what your business is, but as the polite small-talk petered out I explained that I was British, and had come to enquire about a gun-battle that I thought had taken place near here ten years ago. The youth grinned at me, showing crooked teeth. 'There was such a battle,' he said at once. 'I was only a boy then, but my family was living here at the time.'

A pulse of hope shot through me. If this boy's family had been here in 1991, there was a good chance they knew all about Bravo Two Zero. 'Can you tell me what happened?' I asked.

He shook his head. 'There were some foreign commandos hiding in the wadi,' he said. 'And my uncle saw them.'

'Your uncle? I understood it was a shepherd-boy who saw them.'

'All I know is that there was shooting – I only heard about it from my Uncle Abbas. He isn't here today but he will be back tomorrow. He can tell you all you want to know.'

It was tantalizing, but for the moment I had to be content with that.


AFTER DARK, WHILE THE MINDERS, film-crew and drivers put their tents up on a patch of flat ground near the road, I made my way to the LUP and rolled out my sleeping-bag and poncho, intending to spend the night there. Perhaps no one, not even a

shepherd, had slept here since 24 January 1991, when this place had last been home to Bravo Two Zero. As I lay in pitch darkness, on the same patch of rock Vince Phillips or one of the others must have lain on, I tried to imagine them all around me, and the subtle interplay of energies that characterizes any human group. Although SAS men are selected partly for their ability to get on with others in closed environments, given their highly competitive nature, personality clashes are inevitable. McNab's description in his autobiography of how satisfied he was to see others failing on selection, since it meant he was doing well, is probably typical: 'There are more schemers in the SAS than an outsider might think,' Peter Ratcliffe has written. 'Guys just hoping you'll fall, and not at all unwilling to give you that little shove if they can get away with it.'[7] Vince was an outsider who had been posted in from A Squadron to take the second-in-command's slot that would otherwise have gone to Ryan, as the next senior in rank after McNab. Although SAS men feel great loyalty to the Regiment, and a sense of brotherhood that is born of a common mystique and shared hardship, in practice it is the squadron to which they feel their deepest loyalty – a loyalty that has been described by some as taking the place of religion. There is a certain xenophobia against other squadrons: the feeling that their members are 'not quite one of us'. Although McNab praises Ryan's character in his book, calling him 'one of the most purposeful men I'd ever met', he also told the Phillips family privately that he considered him 'the least experienced man in the patrol'. Since Ryan was a corporal with six years in the regular SAS behind him at that time, plus at least four years in the SAS reserve, this opinion is hard to support – McNab himself had been in the Regiment only eight years, and Ryan's total service in both 22 and 23 SAS actually exceeded his.

McNab also contradicts himself to some extent by describing Ryan as the patrol's most experienced medic. Again, one suspects an element of competition here on McNab's part – Ryan was ex-23 SAS and there is no one a regular SAS man resents more than a territorial SAS man. Other units he might look down on from a great height, but the territorial SAS man is like him and yet unlike – the younger brother whose precociousness sticks in the craw. 22 SAS was spawned by a territorial unit, 21 SAS (Artists), which is the senior of the three SAS units, and both 21 and 23 contain some superb soldiers with as much experience as anyone in 22 SAS, whom they have joined on operations from Borneo to Dhofar. The difference is that to apply for TA selection, no parent unit is required. Most regular SAS men define themselves by their parent units: on their vehicle-borne patrols in Iraq, the men of D and A Squadrons even divided themselves up according to whether they were ex-paras (sixty per cent of the Regiment), ex-infantry or ex-service arms. While McNab was proud to have served in the Royal Green Jackets, Ryan had no real parent unit at all. As an entrant straight from the TA, he was – to a greater extent than McNab even – one hundred per cent proof SAS, but to his mates in B Squadron he would probably always remain 'the weekend soldier'. That Ryan felt the need to live this down is suggested by the description of the way he asserts himself in his book, noting that he emerged as the natural 2i/c because he was 'more positive' than Vince on the ground, and that he took up the position of lead scout simply because he 'didn't trust anyone else to go first'.[8] As well as his critical attitude to Phillips, he also points a derogatory finger at his patrol commander, McNab, hinting that on first arrival he was 'semi-stunned' by the enormity of the task, and later, that he was so desperate to prove himself that he devised a

madcap plan to bump an anti-aircraft position that had no relation to their task, and from which Ryan had to gently dissuade him. McNab does not mention the plan, nor does Ryan, in McNab's book, seem to have played the dominating role in decision-making he appears to do in his own. In fact, McNab refers to Vince Phillips as a major player far more than he refers to Ryan. There is an air of knowing best about Ryan's attitude, a sense of the perfectionist loner, 'the voice of reason', as McNab himself puts it. Ryan probably looked down on McNab – an ex-boy soldier – as someone who had been institutionalized by the army, had missed out on the realities of life, and was too 'gobby' – a flaw that had, in fact, very nearly cost him the SAS selection – 'words came out of him so fast,' Ryan said, 'that you never quite knew where you were.' [9]

As I lay there in the LUP, staring at the stars, I also thought about the tremendous loads the patrol had brought in with them, which McNab says they had carried twenty kilometres to this LUP. Each man had a Bergen rucksack – the standard SAS issue, with a capacity of about 100 litres, packed with at least 25 kilos of sandbags and OP equipment per man, rations for ten days, spare batteries for the radio, demolition gear, mines, jerrycans of water, and intravenous drips and fluids for emergencies. The most vital piece of kit was the PRC 319, a state-of-the-art patrol radio with a burst capacity, which meant that encrypted messages could be sent in a fraction of a second and thus reduce the risk of being DF'd (Direction Found) by enemy tracking-stations. The set was an improvement on the old ones only from the point of view of security – the system of using vocabularies and coding the messages on a one-time pad remained as time-consuming as always. The 319 worked on a duplex antenna, a coil of wire that was normally hidden in trees, but would also work when

laid on rocks, the length of which had to be adjusted according to the frequency. Spare antennae were carried so that if the patrol had to move quickly the set could be detached and the antenna in use dumped. The patrol also had with it a field telephone system designed for use between two OPs, and four TACBEs, miniature radio beacons that, when primed, could send a signal to AWACS – the airborne warning and control systems aircraft that coordinated the communications networks and were recognisable by their mushroom-shaped antennae. TACBE was supposed to be able to elicit a response from AWACS within fifteen seconds, and could also be used for contacting aircraft or for ground-to-ground contact at close quarters. In addition to their Bergens, the patrol had belt-kit containing emergency rations, cooking gear and ammunition, and each man had two sandbags filled with extra rations and the crucial NBC (nuclear, biological and chemical warfare) suits comprising two hermetically sealed sets of charcoal-lined smocks and pants, and a gasmask, overboots and gloves. Mobile toilets were not forgotten – in the form of a 'piss can' into which the patrol would urinate, and plastic bags into which they would defecate, carrying all their waste products with them until they could be disposed of safely. Four of the team had M16 Armalite rifles with underslung 40mm grenade-launchers known as M203s, and the others carried Minimis: Belgian-made light machine-guns firing 5.56mm ammunition from both belt and magazine. All had one-shot disposable LAW 66mm rocket-launchers capable of taking out armoured vehicles, L2 High Explosive grenades and white phosphorus grenades. Vince Phillips had a Browning 9mm pistol. Most of the patrol had a poncho or space-blanket, but none had a sleeping-bag – a potentially fatal omission in the icy conditions they encountered. Though McNab states that a

sleeping-bag was a luxury item, such macho aplomb runs counter to everything taught in the Regiment, where no detail of personal morale is neglected. A man who is freezing to death and unable to sleep because of the cold is hardly likely to be able to carry out his task, no matter how many millions of dollars-worth of technology is at his disposal. In the Iraqi desert in winter, a sleeping-bag was definitely not a luxury, but a relatively cheap and light piece of equipment that could have saved lives. The reason Bravo Two Zero did not carry them was not because they were considered luxuries, but because they had not learned the lessons of T.E. Lawrence: they believed that the desert was a hot place, and thought they would simply not need them.

With such a vast amount of equipment to carry about, of course, Bravo Two Zero were at a tremendous disadvantage as a foot patrol. According to ex-RSM Peter Ratcliffe, they had forgotten the Regiment's tradition of travelling fast and light: 'I admit to being the traditional kind of practical soldier who believes you don't need much equipment to operate efficiently,' he wrote, 'and that you should go in as light as possible. But they were taking twenty or thirty bulging sandbags in addition to the rest of their gear.'[10] The day before the operation, Ratcliffe had attempted in vain to try to get McNab to reduce the amount of kit. 'I knew to a certainty they were taking too much,' he wrote. 'I gave them a dozen paces maximum – yet McNab expected them to move freely, as circumstances demanded. An SAS unit, to misquote Mohammed Ali, should be capable of floating like a butterfly and stinging like a swarm of killer bees. The guys in "McNab's" patrol were carrying far too much equipment and far too much weight to be able to operate effectively.'[11]

I awoke in the night to find myself being attacked, not by a

swarm of killer-bees but of midges, and moved my sleeping-bag up to the channel above the wadi. For a while I lay awake, thinking over what I had read in McNab's and Ryan's books about their first day in this LUP, and it seemed to me that things had gone downhill fast from the start. On arriving here not long before first light on 23 January, the patrol had immediately gone to ground, leaving two men on stag, changing every two hours. The weather was much colder than the spring day in England they had anticipated, and by now they must have realized that lying hidden for hours on OP in these temperatures was going to be no joke. Second, and more serious from the point of view of their task, they now knew it would be impossible to put in their observation post because the ground was rock-hard rather than sandy. They had practised digging the OP in the Empty Quarter of southern Arabia – the world's largest sand desert – and had mistakenly expected the texture of the desert to be similar here. This meant that they had expended energy and resources in lugging along material for building the OP which had turned out to be totally wasted.

When first light came, they checked down the wadi to make sure they had left no tracks, and set up two Claymore anti-personnel mines at fifty metres – basically, shaped charges of PE with ball-bearings embedded in them. The mines were operated by clackers on the end of wires and could be used to spray a path or route if anyone tried to approach them. McNab did a recce, saw the house nearby and, realizing they were too close to habitation for comfort, wrote a sitrep (situation report) which Legs, the 'Scaley', or signaller, encrypted and typed into the 319, then sent off. There was no acknowledgement. Again and again they tried, changing the shape and length of the antenna and recalibrating frequencies, but with no result. By the

end of the day, the patrol accepted that they had lost comms. This was the most perilous blow they had received so far, because without radio contact they were cut off from their base almost 320 kilometres (two hundred miles) away. McNab remained cool, however, because they had a prearranged lost comms procedure, by which, if nothing was heard from them, the helicopter would return to the original drop-off point in exactly 48 hours.

There was worse news to come that night, however, when McNab discovered a nest of two S60 anti-aircraft guns on the ridge north of the road, which he says were attended by Iraqi troops in platoon strength. The following day, he says, he spotted yet another pair of S60s, only three hundred metres from the LUP, and for the first time he started to feel jittery. There was still no go on the 319, so the patrol prepared themselves to move back to the heli rendezvous that night.

Meanwhile, though, Ryan says, McNab made plans to attack the AA position (he does not make clear which one), intending to slam it with everything they had, then make a run for it back to the helicopter RV. Ryan was incensed, pointing out that whatever installation the AA guns were guarding, it had to be protected by large numbers of troops, and anyway, to knock out AA guns was not part of their remit: 'Our operation's here in the OP,' Ryan told him. 'If we can't stay here we'd better go back.'[12] By 1400 hours McNab had dropped the idea of attacking the guns and decided they would simply move back to the RV and wait for the heli to come in. It was as they were preparing to move out, both claim, that the patrol was compromised.

Although McNab and Ryan describe the compromise differently, both agree that it was a shepherd-boy who spotted them.

McNab writes that at about 1600 hours the patrol heard goat-bells approaching the LUP from the west – the direction of the house. Shortly afterwards, a small boy appeared at the lip of the wadi and saw them sitting there. Astonished, McNab implies he immediately made off towards the AA emplacement the patrol had clocked earlier. McNab notes that both Vince and Mark attempted to run after the boy, but had given up the idea for fear of being noticed by the AA gunners. Accepting that Bravo Two Zero had been compromised, McNab then gave the order to pull out.

According to Ryan, the shepherd-boy would not have noticed them except for the fact that, overcome with the temptation to see what was happening, Vince Phillips moved, craning his head to see if he could spot him. At the time, though, Ryan says, no one was sure if the boy had really seen them at all – it was only later that Vince came clean about it. In Ryan's version, there is no mad rush towards the AA guns, and no desperate attempt by Vince and Mark to intercept the youth. Ryan says that there was no cry of alarm and that *it was pretty obvious that the boy had run off* (italics mine), which is merely an assumption, not an observed fact, while McNab recounts that he actually made eye contact with the boy and saw the astonishment in his eyes, and that the youth suddenly went running off. McNab also writes that he 'followed the boy with his eyes' as he ran away, yet the LUP is five metres deep and steep-sided, and while you could see someone standing right on the lip, it would be impossible for men lying prone to have seen the boy running off. Not only does McNab's account seem unlikely judging by the ground, but the two accounts are obviously incompatible. I looked forward keenly to returning to the farm the following day, hoping that some fresh light would be shed on the matter by the mysterious 'Uncle Abbas'.

# CHAPTER
# SIX

ABBAS BIN FADHIL WAS THE head of the extended family living in the settlement on the hill – a family that must have numbered at least thirty men, women and children. He was a slim, upright man with an open face and a wild beard, who walked with a pronounced limp. His voice was raucous and he tended to shout, as Bedouin will do, but he exuded warmth and hospitality. As I shook hands with him and his relatives and seated myself on a cushion in the vast mudhif or reception room, I wondered what the day would bring.

Abbas ordered tea for everyone, and while it was being served I gazed around me. There were no electric lights in this place, I noted, and neither did there appear to be any running water. The house consisted of little more than this mudhif, carpeted and lined with cushions – obviously no one but guests actually slept there. While we were drinking the tea, Abbas introduced me to two more Bedouin:

a tall, spindly-looking man with a Mexican-style moustache, a little younger than Abbas himself, and a handsome youth of about eighteen or twenty. The tall man was Abbas's younger brother, Hayil, and the youth their nephew, Adil. As we chatted, Abbas told me that they belonged to a Bedouin tribe called the Buhayat, who had long had a farm in the area. Though he had been brought up in a black tent in the desert and had ridden camels as a boy, his family were now settled here. They raised livestock – mainly sheep – and planted wheat in the wadis after the rains, but had long ago given up their camels in favour of motor vehicles.

Abbas said that the mudhif we were sitting in was new, but it stood on the site of a more primitive structure which had been hit by Allied bombers back in 1991. 'Thank God no one was killed,' he said. 'But they did hit some Bedouin tents on other raids and killed both people and sheep. Now what was the point of that?' Despite the fact that I was British, he appeared – like the people in Baghdad – to nurse no grievance against me personally. 'I can tell you everything about the foreign soldiers who were here,' he said. 'At the time we thought they were Americans, but if you say they were British, all right. First of all, it wasn't a herdsboy who saw them in the wadi, it was me. I was the one who saw them first.'

I squinted at Abbas, wondering whether he might have been mistaken for a boy ten years before. Black-bearded and weathered-looking, I concluded that he was a man who had probably looked forty all his adult life. Excited, I watched him, waiting for more, but he suddenly urged me up and called me outside. 'There's something I must show you,' he said.

Behind the house was a square of one-roomed stone cottages, which were evidently the real living quarters of the house, and

a large open-sided barn. There were three vehicles in the barn: a battered truck and two yellow bulldozers. Abbas led me to the larger of the bulldozers. 'I bought this new back in the 1980s,' he said. 'Imported direct from Japan. In 1991 there was a very cold winter. The wind was terrible. This house is on a hill, as you can see, so one day – it was 24 January; I know the date because a lot happened on that day – I decided to park it down in the wadi, out of the wind. I was afraid the fuel would freeze up. I drove it down there – it only takes a few minutes from the house – and right up to the end of the wadi, where there is a sheltered place. When I got there I saw two armed men peering at me over the rocks, not more than ten metres away, one on the side of the wadi in front of me and one below to my left. They were wearing camouflage jackets and shamaghs over their faces, and I had no idea who they were. They could have been Iraqi commandos, or special troops of the Intelligence Service, or enemy fliers who had crashed. They could have been sheep-rustlers. Whoever they were, I decided to pretend I hadn't seen them. I looked at the ground, avoided eye contact, and reversed the bulldozer out of the wadi-end. Then I just turned it round and drove straight back to the house.'

I listened to Abbas, fascinated. Both McNab and Ryan had described a man approaching them on a bulldozer, but I hadn't mentioned it either to Abbas or to the youth last night. It had come entirely out of the blue. Now it appeared I had not only found the driver they had written about, but the bulldozer too.

McNab recalls that the patrol had heard the sound of a tracked vehicle and, assuming it was an armoured personnel carrier alerted by the herdsboy, had cocked their 66mm rocket-launchers, ready to take it out. When it had come into view and McNab saw that it was

just 'an idiot pottering about with a digger' he had relaxed, thinking – rightly, according to Abbas – that it was there quite innocently. McNab had been wrong, though, in assuming that 'the idiot' hadn't seen them – in fact, Abbas's quick thinking in averting his gaze had probably saved his life. Ryan writes that the patrol knew the man had spotted them, concluding that since the wadi was a cul-de-sac he could only have been coming to find out who was there. This in turn suggested that the shepherd-boy had warned him.

When I asked Abbas about this, he laughed and pointed at Adil, his nephew. 'There's your shepherd-boy,' he said. 'Ask him.'

As I turned to him in surprise, Adil explained that he had been out herding sheep (not goats, as McNab and Ryan said) the same afternoon. 'I was about ten years old then,' he said. 'I took the sheep up to the wadi edge, but I didn't go down into it. It is true that I looked down into the wadi, but I certainly didn't see any foreign soldiers there. I know now they were there, of course, but I didn't see them at the time, and didn't know anything about it until my uncle told me later.'

I was bowled over by Adil's revelation. Here, against all the odds, was the very boy who would remain frozen for all time in McNab's and Ryan's books as the shepherd who had spotted them and ultimately brought about their downfall. And yet, according to the shepherd-boy's own testimony, he had not seen them at all.

Couldn't it have been someone else, I insisted? Surely Adil wasn't the only boy herding sheep that day?

'If someone else had seen them, they would have come straight to us,' Abbas said, 'as our house is so near to the wadi. One way or another we would have heard about it, at the time, or since. Everyone who lives in the desert here is related to us – this is the tribal area of

the Buhayat. There aren't any strangers around and no one herds sheep here except our family. All I can say is if there was another boy who saw the commandos, then he certainly didn't tell anyone.'

It made sense: this was a remote desert region, not a busy city street full of nameless faces. I knew from experience how efficient and precise the Bedouin grapevine could be – if another herdsboy *had* seen Bravo Two Zero, Abbas and his family would certainly have known.

I remembered McNab had written that the boy might have gone running off to tell the anti-aircraft gunners, and I asked Abbas if there had been any S60s in the area at the time. He pointed to the high ridge running along the road about four hundred metres away. 'There was an anti-aircraft post up there,' he said. 'But with only a few soldiers. We had nothing to do with them at all. The nearest military base was about fifteen kilometres away across the plateau. The soldiers up there had no vehicles – they were dropped off and picked up by vehicles from the base, and they wouldn't have left their post anyway. Why would Adil go to the anti-aircraft guns – even assuming he had seen the commandos in the wadi, which he hadn't – instead of coming to his family? He was only a small boy. It doesn't make sense.'

I asked Abbas to take me in the bulldozer to reconstruct the short journey of that day ten years ago, and as we trundled up the narrow, steep-sided wadi to the LUP, I experienced a deep thrill. Here I was, seeing not what McNab and Ryan had seen as they peered through the sights of their 66s and Minimi light machine-guns that day, but, incredibly, what the 'idiot in the digger' had seen, sitting on the same bulldozer with the man himself.

Both McNab and Ryan had written that the bulldozer had

stopped 150 metres from their position, but on the ground I could see this was clearly a mistake, because the LUP was tucked behind a bend in the wadi. Unless the patrol had left their LUP, then they could not have seen the vehicle at such a distance, and indeed, both texts suggest they saw the bulldozer only when it came round a corner. Abbas showed me where he had stopped – almost close enough to the LUP to spit – and pointed out where the two men had been.

As we drove back to the house, bumping over the stones, I wondered if Abbas and Adil were telling the truth. I knew that Bedouin do not lie, but under enough pressure from the government, they might have had no choice. Yet no one in the government had known I was coming here to this particular spot, and no one had suggested it. If I had followed Ali's advice, we would have ended up somewhere completely different – even Uday at the Ministry of Information had told me it was highly unlikely I would find eyewitnesses. Any campaign of disinformation would have involved deliberately putting me off-guard with a Machiavellian system of feints and double-bluffs, insisting I would find no witnesses, but with success dependent on the notion that I would find them anyway. And for Abbas, from his Bedouin's point of view, what would be the point of lying? Why, in a culture where the cult of reputation rules supreme, should Abbas deny that his nephew had spotted the patrol if it were the truth, and why should Adil connive in that lie? On the other hand, whether Adil had seen the patrol or not was crucial to my purpose – one I had not even revealed to the Bedouin. If the boy had not spotted anyone, as he claimed, then Vince Phillips could not have compromised the patrol as Ryan and the classified report suggest.

# CHAPTER
# seven

AFTER ABBAS HAD RETURNED his bulldozer into the barn, I asked him to explain what had happened on 24 January 1991 after he had spotted the British patrol. In reply, he led me back down towards the site of the LUP, with Hayil and Adil following on. As we walked across the slightly undulating landscape, Abbas hobbling on his crippled ankle, I began to glimpse the desert as they saw it. The area Bravo Two Zero had chosen to lie up in was this family's backyard. Given Bedouin powers of observation and the very proximity of the place, there had really been no more chance of the SAS escaping unseen than if a band of Iraqis had landed on a British council estate. Was McNab right, then, to blame the Head Shed for the compromise because they were dropped in inhabited country, in the middle of more than 3500 Iraqi troops?

According to McNab's own text, the patrol alone picked the

place on the MSR where they would insert their LUP. They also decided to be flown in by Chinook rather than driving or going on foot, and selected the dropping-off place themselves. To choose a point twenty kilometres from the site of the LUP when you are carrying 95 kilos of gear looks like unsound strategy, but McNab explains this by saying that he didn't want the heli to be compromised by locals. At the same time, he says that the house 'shouldn't have been there', and that they had been dropped in an area as crowded as Piccadilly Circus: it is difficult to see how he could have been afraid of being compromised by locals he didn't know were there, especially when he adds that the object was to reach the LUP as quickly as possible.[13] According to the blurb of McNab's book, supported by his sketch-map, the patrol lugged their equipment – Bergens, belt-kit, jerrycans of water and two full sandbags apiece – twenty kilometres, in the dark over unknown, hostile country, in only nine hours. Anyone who has tried to carry 95, or even 80 kilos any distance, even in daylight, will recognize this as no mean feat of endurance. To make things doubly difficult, half of the team had to be protecting the others as they moved, so every few hundred metres they had to dump what they had shifted and go back for more – which would presumably have taken twice the time. If it is true that the SAS men patrolled twenty kilometres across flat desert to reach their objective carrying such burdens, as the blurb of Bravo Two Zero states, then it is rightly celebrated. The question is, did it really happen in the first place?

I asked Abbas how he thought the enemy patrol had arrived in the area. 'They came by helicopter,' he told me confidently. 'In fact, we heard it come in, at about eight o'clock on 22 January. I remember the time because I sent someone to the nearest military base to

report it. I knew it was a twin-engined helicopter by the sound, but of course at the time I wasn't sure whether it was one of theirs or one of ours. It landed not more than two kilometres from the house – I know that for certain because we found the tracks later. It was very muddy then and the tracks were clear – big wheels, you couldn't mistake it. In fact the tracks stayed there for weeks until the rain washed them away, and everybody here saw them.'

I asked what the military had done when his messenger had reported the aircraft. 'They didn't investigate it,' he said, 'because they thought it was one of ours. It was only later we connected it with the foreign commandos and realized it must have brought them in.'

He showed me a flat-bottomed wadi where he had found the Chinook's tracks, and I later measured it with the Magellan as about two kilometres south of the LUP. If Abbas was telling the truth, it meant the feat made so much of in the blurb of McNab's book was incorrect. Moreover, if the patrol had really reached their objective at 0445 hours on 23 January, as McNab said, it had taken them just under nine hours to ferry their kit two kilometres – a feat of a far more mundane, but also more reasonable order.

I tried carrying four twenty-litre jerrycans – a total weight of eighty kilos – a distance of one kilometre, and with pauses for rest it took an agonizing hour. Of course, the SAS patrol were much younger and fitter than me, but even if they managed to do it in half the time, it would still have taken ten hours to cover twenty kilometres, assuming each man was carrying his own kit. But we know this was not so, because McNab points out that they used a shuttle system, and in fact only half the patrol was carrying at any one time – bringing the time to twenty hours: more than double what McNab says.

Two kilometres though, would be a comfortable distance to carry such weights in nine hours, silently and tactically, with appropriate rests and time to scout the country ahead as well. The fact that Abbas said the heli came in only two kilometres away is doubly interesting, because it not only coincides with what Ryan wrote, but would also explain why McNab had seen a settlement with water-tower at both the helicopter drop-off point and the LUP – Abbas's house could be seen from both. Incidentally, the fact that the helicopter was heard is inadvertently revealed in McNab's book when one of his interrogators tells him so, and as for his assertion that according to the intelligence officer's briefing, the house 'should not have been there', Ryan clearly states that the satellite images they had been shown revealed crops and habitation.

We halted on the flat ground opposite the overhanging rock shelf of the LUP and Abbas pointed down into the cul-de-sac. 'It was from here that I saw them for the second time,' he said. 'But that time I was armed. When I got back to the house with the bulldozer I went straight in and got my AK47. While I was loading it, my father, Fadhil – who is dead now, may God have mercy upon him – asked me what I was doing. "I've seen some strangers in the wadi," I told him. "I don't know who they are – whether they are Iraqi army or foreigners or bandits – but I'm going to find out what they're doing." I wasn't really concerned with the war at that stage – it didn't enter my mind. I was only worried because there were these armed strangers near my home, where there were women and children. I was afraid some harm would come to my family. My father was over seventy then, but he insisted on coming with me. He got out his old rifle. It was a Brno five-shot, one of the old type with the bolt action that you have to cock shot by shot. It was almost as old as

he was. Then, as he was getting his rifle out, my brother Hayil arrived and asked what was up. We told him and he said, "I'm coming too," and got out his AK47. So we were three – me, my brother and my father.'

Abbas pointed again to the watershed, about five metres below us. 'When we got to this point, I saw eight men down there. I suspected they were foreigners, but I still couldn't tell for certain. They saw me, but I was holding my AK47 down by my side so they couldn't see it.' (In fact, Ryan notes that he saw the Arabs holding the rifles by their sides.)

'Why didn't you attack them then and there?' I asked. 'They would have been sitting ducks.'

'There were two reasons. First we only had rifles, and there were rocks to hide behind in that wadi. They could have got behind the rocks and we would never have been able to kill them. There were eight of them and only three of us – my father was an old man, and I have a crippled ankle and can't run, so we wanted to be sure of our ground before we did anything. The second thing was we still didn't know who they were, and if we'd shot them and they turned out to be Iraqis we could have got into big trouble. Remember, they'd seen us but hadn't done anything, and it's very hard to just shoot someone down in cold blood, whoever they are. So for now we just watched.

'Soon – it was late afternoon, about five-thirty or so – they started moving south down the wadi in single file. They were carrying packs that looked very heavy, and were spaced about ten metres apart. We didn't do anything, but just walked parallel with them along the wadi to see where they would go.'

He led me along the edge of the wadi on the same route, where

the hooves of thousands of sheep and goats had cut grooves in the surface over generations. As we went, I tried to imagine how it must have felt for both parties – British and Arab – one above, one below, both knowing the other was there, but not yet certain they were hostile. For the SAS, I guessed, the strain must have been almost unbearable.

Although some of the men in Bravo Two Zero, like Vince Phillips, were veterans, this was their first operation in a 'real war'. Several of the team – perhaps most – had been involved in operations in Northern Ireland, but those were security operations rather than genuine combat. This was the Big One they had all been waiting for. They might have fought terrorists, but none of the team – not even McNab – had been involved in a real firefight against superior numbers of troops, and they were asking themselves, perhaps, how they and their comrades would react.

'This was what we were there for,' Peter Ratcliffe wrote, 'what all the years of training were about. However useful we had proved ourselves in dealing with terrorists, only in a war could we ever put our training to full use and only in a war would we get the chance to prove conclusively that we were worth our pay.'[14] They were selected SAS soldiers – the finest Special Forces men in the world – but as Ratcliffe has pointed out, 'Selection doesn't tell you everything you need to know about a man. Only what he does in battle will ever show you what he's really like.'[15] They were a tiny unit in a hostile environment, without transport and without communications. The infiltration with so much equipment must have been incredibly tense, and on top of the revelation that the ground was too hard to dig an OP had come the realization that the radio wouldn't work, and finally, that there were anti-aircraft guns almost on top of

73

the LUP. As they moved out that afternoon, watching the Arabs for the first move in a drama that must inevitably come, the tension among the patrol members must have been like a taut bowstring waiting for release.

I saw that the wadi was flattening out into a basin five or six hundred metres wide, rimmed by stony shale outcrops on both sides. The basin was grassy, with a few stunted thorn-bushes, and to the west the desert stretched away in galleries of serrated humpbacks as far as the eye could see. Abbas led me over to the eastern side of the basin, nearest to his house, which was still in full view. The place where he claimed to have found the Chinook tracks lay less than a kilometre to the south. 'This is where we were when they came out of the wadi,' he said. 'We waited for them to come one by one. There were eight of them and I remember the last but one – the seventh – actually waved at us.'

I was intensely interested in this point because I remembered that Ryan wrote that he had waved at the Arabs, though he also said that he had been first in the file, not seventh. Hayil, Abbas's brother, confirmed that it was the seventh man who had waved, but neither could remember if the man had used his left or right hand. This was significant also, because Ryan said that by waving with his left hand he inadvertently revealed to the watching Arabs that the patrol were Christians. An Arab, he writes, will never wave with his left hand, which is considered unclean. While it is true that Bedouin use their left hands to clean themselves after defecating, a left-hand wave has no particular significance, and evidently it meant nothing to Abbas and Hayil.

Nevertheless, the detail was important, for if these Bedouin had somehow been got at and briefed by the Iraqi government, why

would they be so insistent that it was the seventh man who waved, when Ryan is adamant in his book that he was in the lead? Since no spin could be put in the waver's position, wouldn't they have left this insignificant detail intact in order to convince me of their veracity? The question was, who was right: these Bedouin or Ryan? Turning to McNab's book, I thought I might have the solution. McNab writes clearly that Ryan was placed in the lead only after the patrol had been ambushed, when he changed the order of march. This suggests that wherever Ryan might have been in the line-up as they moved out of the LUP, he was not the first man, as he says.

'They were moving fast,' Abbas said, 'and we knew we had to do something before they got away, but we still didn't know who they were. We decided to fire two warning shots over their heads to find out who they were.'

At first I wondered what he meant. Then I remembered that, in the past, when Bedouin tribes used to raid each other for camels, they were often faced with the same problem of identifying friends or enemies before it was too late. When a party of unknown camel-riders approached a camp, the men there would fire a few shots over their heads. If the strangers were friends they would wave their head-cloths and shout "Afya ! Afya!" (It's all right) in reply, or sometimes throw handfuls of sand in the air.

'I fired two quick shots over the strangers' heads with my AK47' Abbas said, 'and immediately they went down. By God, they were fast. They started shooting back straight away, so of course we knew they were enemies. We were lying flat out on the ground about three hundred metres from them, and had taken off our red shamaghs so as not to present good targets. It must have been quite difficult for

them to see exactly where we were. Hayil and I were putting down fire on automatic and my father was struggling with his old rifle. Suddenly they fired rockets in our direction – two rounds, which just exploded harmlessly in the desert. At the time I thought they were mortar shells, but later we found the used rocket-launchers.'

'What happened then?'

'A smoke grenade went up, or maybe more than one, and under the cover of the smoke they pulled out. From what we could see they seemed to do it in a very disciplined way, working in pairs with one firing and the other retreating. We were still firing, but couldn't see them properly until they went over the rim of that ridge, heading south-west. Actually, we only saw five of them going over the hill, and we thought maybe we'd hit the other three.'

I listened to Abbas's tale with growing incredulity, waiting in vain for the point when the hordes of Iraqi troops and vehicles mentioned by McNab and Ryan would turn up. In McNab's book, the patrol is attacked by two armoured personnel carriers with 7.62mm machine-guns, and at least three lorry-loads of Iraqi troops and two Land-Cruisers. Coming under fire from the APCs and hordes of infantry, and amidst a great deal of screaming, 'Let's do it!', McNab's patrol fires off its 66mm rocket-launchers, dumps its heavy Bergens and charges the APCs, putting them out of action and killing or wounding dozens of Iraqis with their Minimi machine-guns and M203 grenade-launchers. McNab describes how the ground was littered with writhing bodies, and how Iraqi casualties were spread over a wide area – 'fifteen dead and many more wounded', he recounts. A burned-out APC smoulders and a truck blazes, with a black and peeling Iraqi lolling in the passenger seat. Someone lobs an L2 grenade through the unbattened

door of one of the APCs, killing dozens more. 'The troops that withdrew were sort of reorganizing themselves,' he explained later to one newspaper. 'It was very much like a scenario in a school playground where you would get two gangs – they would have a fight, one gang would run away and then sort of poke their fingers out, "We're going to get you." And then they'd sort themselves out and come forward again. Now, we didn't want to get involved in that, so we ran . . .'

According to the book, having reduced the Iraqi ambush to bloody ribbons, McNab's patrol withdraws, picks up its Bergens and makes off over the brow of the hill, where it comes under concentrated fire from the S60 anti-aircraft battery on the ridge nearby and is forced to drop its Bergens once again. As more enemy vehicles roll up, the patrol disappears into the growing dark.

If there was no trace of McNab's pitched battle against massively superior forces in Abbas's and Hayil's accounts, what about Ryan, I wondered? Initially, in fact, his description bears some resemblance to what they told me. He writes that he saw two (not three) Arabs pacing them down the wadi, but hoped that they would go away. When he waved, though, the Arabs opened fire, and shortly afterwards, a tipper-truck arrived with eight or ten soldiers in it. In Ryan there is no long build-up with tracked vehicles approaching ominously, heard but not seen, nor is there a salvo of rockets as the patrol takes them on. Ryan does declare that Stan had seen an APC, but that somehow he'd failed to notice it, as it was 'probably behind a mound'. In his account there are no writhing bodies, and while McNab states 'fifteen dead and many more wounded', Ryan puts the total number of Iraqis after them as 'about a dozen', three of whom he accounts for himself. Significantly, in Ryan's book, the

patrol does not charge, but simply drops its Bergens and makes off over the ridge, where it comes under anti-aircraft fire. A bullet narrowly misses Ryan's arm and knocks his Bergen flat (McNab says it was an anti-aircraft shell), but, undeterred, he goes back for a hip-flask of whisky his wife had given him as a Christmas present – an exploit also repeated by McNab.

Again and again I pressed Abbas and Hayil on the subject of armoured personnel carriers, vehicles and Iraqi troops, desperate to find some reference to them, no matter how oblique. 'There were no personnel carriers,' they repeated, 'and no troops. There were only the three of us, no one else at all.' Abbas stated over and over that there had been no pitched battle, and that the action had all been over in five minutes or so. 'I fired four magazines,' he told me. 'About 120 rounds.'

'I fired about eighty,' Hayil added. 'I don't know how many my father fired, but not many because his rifle was old.'

If these Bedouin were telling the truth, then McNab's 'colossal amount of fire' consisted of a total of about two hundred rounds.

Abbas beckoned me towards the humpbacked ridge on the brow of which he had last seen five members of the SAS patrol. 'They ran off south-west,' he said. 'And believe me, they were really moving fast.' The Bedouin showed me where they had found the Bergens dumped by the SAS, in two groups. 'There were eight packs,' Abbas said. 'Really big things, they were. But we didn't open them as I thought they might be booby-trapped. We decided not to try to follow them because it was getting dark, and anyhow, I can't walk far with my bad leg. If we had wanted to, some of our people could have tracked them easily enough, as the ground was quite greasy, but we were defending our home, and the main thing was that they'd gone.

When the Iraqi army came later, they did open the packs and they found all sorts of stuff – a radio, medical equipment, food, a flag and a map – everything you can think of. But at the time all we found here apart from the packs was a clip of tracer rounds, spent rocket-launcher cases, and a pool of blood.'

I pricked my ears up at this. There was no indication in either McNab's or Ryan's accounts that any of the patrol had been injured during the attack. 'Are you sure it was blood?' I asked. Both Hayil and Abbas assured me that it was, and I put this down as another mystery. Obviously the Bedouin were quite anxious to establish the fact that they had hit someone, and they were a little crestfallen when I said that as far as I knew, none of the patrol had been hurt. They had engaged Bravo Two Zero at three hundred metres – the extreme effective range of the AK47, which is anyway a notoriously difficult weapon to fire lying down because the magazine is too long. Had the brothers simply invented the blood to reinforce their reputation as marksmen, I wondered, or had one of the patrol actually been injured running away and had somehow kept it quiet?

As we climbed to the top of the ridge over which the SAS had fled, I quizzed them about the anti-aircraft guns both Ryan and McNab said had opened up on them as they cleared it. The two Arabs shook their heads emphatically. 'The anti-aircraft guns never opened fire,' Abbas said, nodding towards the ridge on which the battery had stood, now about a kilometre away. 'The soldiers up there wouldn't have known what was happening – even we didn't realize these were enemy troops until we fired the warning shots. How would we have contacted the battery? We had no radio. The anti-aircraft guns were there to protect the base across the plateau

from enemy aircraft, not for fighting on the ground. Anyway, it all happened so quickly – there just wouldn't have been time for the gunners to realize what was happening and open fire.'

When I explained that McNab said an AA round had passed through Ryan's Bergen, Abbas chortled. 'Are you joking ?' he asked. 'You must know that an S60 shell is a huge thing - 57mm - as big around as a Coca-Cola can. It's designed for destroying aeroplanes. If one of them hit your pack, there wouldn't be much of it left.'

'What about the Iraqi army ?' I asked. 'When did they turn up ?'

'We didn't send anyone to tell them until after the foreigners had got away,' Abbas said. 'And the boy I sent had to go on foot, because there was petrol rationing then and we had none for our vehicles. The base was fifteen kilometres away, like I said, so it took him a long time to get there, and by the time the army got themselves sorted out and got here it was one o'clock in the morning (25 January) and the commandos had been gone for hours. There were heavy air attacks all over Iraq that day, and the army were worried that the commandos would call down air strikes if they pursued them, so they left them alone. In fact, we did hear some enemy jets going over between midnight and one in the morning.' This was a point, I noted, that was confirmed by McNab, who was a few kilometres south-west of Abbas's house at around that time, and who tried to contact the Coalition jets on his TACBE.

I thought about it carefully. 'I don't understand,' I said. 'I mean, the AA post was only a kilometre away. Even if the soldiers there didn't open fire with their S60s, surely they would have come to help you, or radioed for more troops.'

'They couldn't leave their post,' Abbas said. 'What if an enemy

aircraft came in on a bombing-run? I don't think they had any radio either, but even if they did report it back, it still took the army hours to get here. Like I said, it was all over within a few minutes – the soldiers wouldn't have had time to work out what was going on.'

In a roasting wind I scoured the battlefield carefully for remnants of the firefight described in McNab's book. I had been travelling in the Middle East long enough to know that if vehicles are knocked out in the desert, no one will bother to clear them up. Sinai, for instance, is still littered with the hulks of scores of armoured vehicles dating from the 1967 war. If Bravo Two Zero had really put two armoured personnel carriers and several trucks out of action, there would almost certainly be debris, and yet there was nothing at all – not a fragment of twisted metal, not a link of track, not a sliver of tyre-rubber, not even a screw. Moreover, the basin was uniformly flat, without a groove, a mound or a fold. If APCs had been there, it would have been impossible not to have seen them, I realized.

Later, back at Abbas's house, I brooded over the mystery. McNab writes with such authority in his book, that it was difficult not to be convinced. Yet my own training in the SAS had taught me that it would be folly for a foot patrol to charge a brace of armoured vehicles. SAS philosophy has always been that nine times out of ten discretion is the better part of valour. The SOP (standard operational procedure) on coming into contact with armour is simply to run away as fast as possible – much as Ryan describes. McNab admitted this himself later in a newspaper interview: 'The last thing you want to do is to start getting involved in any contact of any type. Number one, that's not our task; we're not there to start fighting people. We're not a big force. We're not armed enough for that, that

wasn't our job.' Yet the same man who admitted later to an interviewer, 'The object is not to fight the enemy, it's to get away from them,' says in his book that he led a suicidal charge against enemy armour in defiance not only of SAS principles, but of every rule in the military book. McNab writes that scores of Iraqis were killed or injured in the contact, and even Ryan suggests obliquely to have shot three men. The brothers assured me repeatedly that not one of them was hit. 'Not even a scratch,' as Abbas said.

In the evening they took me back over to the barn, where they showed me some of the artefacts they had retrieved from Bravo Two Zero's cache in the wadi. 'There was a huge amount of equipment there,' Abbas said. 'Clothing, sandbags, shovels, food, jerrycans – even explosives, which the Iraqi army destroyed.' He showed me a shovel and a jerrycan marked with the British MoD arrow that were obviously in use by his family and, later, a clip of 5.56mm orange and green tracer rounds, not used by the Iraqi army, a camouflage net, a gas-mask, and pieces of a Claymore anti-personnel mine that matched the one shown in McNab's book. 'They dug this up in the wadi,' Abbas said. 'And smashed it.' This confirmed McNab's statement that they had deployed two Claymores and buried them in the wadi bed when they pulled out. It was exciting to think that I was holding a historical artefact – the remains of one of the Claymores actually used by Bravo Two Zero and mentioned in McNab's book. I was delighted when Abbas told me I could keep them. I also asked what had happened to the eight Bergens they had found, and the brothers said they had been taken by the army and were probably in Baghdad.

After sunset, the Bedouin slaughtered two sheep in our honour, inviting in all the family and neighbours. A vast oilskin sheet was

rolled out in the guest hall and the food brought in, great brass trays piled with hunks of mutton on buttered rice. We ate the food in Arab fashion, with our right hands, crouching around the trays, and I felt at home once again, basking in the hospitality of these simple people. Afterwards, as we sat replete, sipping tea, Abbas told the Bravo Two Zero story once more in front of everyone, while the other Bedouin nodded as if they had heard it many times before. If this was a set-up, I thought, then either everybody here was in on it, or Abbas and Hayil didn't care that they were known as liars to the world at large. Bearing in mind that lying was taboo in Bedouin society, this seemed highly unlikely. Indeed, Abbas and Hayil's courage in taking on eight men armed with machine-guns and rocket-launchers was totally in keeping with the Bedouin ideal.

'Didn't it bother you that they were more than you and better armed?' I asked.

Abbas shrugged and showed me his crippled ankle, pointing out three or four scars that were obviously bullet entry-wounds. 'That was a machine-gun,' he told me. 'In the Iran-Iraq war I was in the Iraqi Special Forces for twelve years, eight years in the war. I saw hundreds of comrades killed, and was wounded six times. I still have two bullets lodged in my body. They used to use us as snatch-squads, going into the Iranian trenches to bring back Iranians who could be interrogated to give information. We sometimes had to fight with bayonets and – God have mercy on me – I once killed a man with a rock because I had no bullets left. I was promoted to sergeant major, received four citations for bravery, and was once court-martialled because a general ordered my squad to retreat and I refused and called him a donkey and a coward. I got off with it, though. Hayil, my brother, also served in the Special Forces and also received

citations for bravery. I got invalided out of the army because of my ankle and couldn't serve in the war of 1991, but anyhow, we are Bedouin and have been handling firearms all our lives. I shot my first wolf when I was twelve. We are used to protecting our flocks and our families, so taking on eight men wasn't such a big deal to my father, my brother and me.'

Here, I thought, was another incredible layer to the story. If what Abbas told me was correct, then Bravo Two Zero had certainly picked the wrong neighbourhood for their OP. Not only had they been put to flight by an old man, a cripple and his younger brother, but two of those three men had more combat experience between them than the entire strength of the SAS patrol combined.

# CHAPTER
## eight

AS THE SUN SET ON 24 JANUARY, Bravo Two Zero melted into the desert, knowing that they were now hunted men. According to both McNab and Ryan, there were vehicle headlights flashing frantically in their wake and they heard occasional bursts of shooting. Quite unaware that there were two extremely cool and seasoned veterans of the Iraqi Special Forces behind them, McNab assumed that the Iraqis were totally confused and shooting haphazardly at rocks and their own shadows. He confessed himself 'chuffed no end'.

The team had ditched their Bergens and now had to rely on the escape-belts to which SAS culture attaches great importance. Normally these belts should contain ammunition, a foldable Hexamine cooker about the size of a Walkman, some kind of shelter – a poncho, bivvy-bag or space-blanket – mugs, mess-tins, water-bottles, an individualized escape kit containing useful items such as waterproofed

matches, and dry rations for 24 hours. The radio had been dumped, and when McNab asked Legs about it, the patrol signaller replied that it was in his Bergen, which had 'probably been shot to fuck by now anyway'. McNab thought the loss of the radio no problem at all, because they had their four TACBE radio beacons and could get a fifteen-second response from patrolling AWACS, although both he and Ryan had pulled the tabs on their beacons during the contact and no response had yet come. McNab wasn't worried about navigation either, because Coburn ('Mark') had a Magellan GPS unit. What they did not have, though, was what they needed most: motor vehicles.

The Saudi border, beyond which lay their forward operating base (FOB), was about three hundred kilometres to the south, while the Syrian border lay only 178 kilometres to the west. Jordan was nearer than either, but the SAS had been warned not to head there as the Jordanians supported Iraq and had recently handed over a downed American airman to the Iraqis. As the patrol rallied after the attack, McNab says, he decided that their best option was to tab (march) west to Syria, though first they would put in a dog's leg feint to give their pursuers the impression they were going south.

Even disregarding Abbas's and Hayil's testimony that there were no pursuers, and that no Iraqi vehicles turned up until about seven hours after the firefight, McNab's account is problematical. According to his own story, the Chinook was due to fly in at 0400 hours the following morning to the drop-off point, which according to his sketch-map lay twenty kilometres due south. If this was correct, the SAS had at least nine hours to make the helicopter rendezvous – a breeze for an unladen patrol. Why did McNab decide suddenly to

head for Syria if, as far as he knew, the helicopter would be coming in to rendezvous due south of them in nine hours' time? The answer may lie in Ryan's account. If, as Ryan and the Bedouin all testified, the helicopter RV actually lay only a kilometre from the site of the ambush, and if, as Ryan says, it was timed at midnight, then it had now certainly been compromised by the enemy. Had they been able to make the RV unscathed, Ryan thought, they could have held off the enemy till nightfall, but if the Chinook came in now, it would be spotted by the Iraqis and perhaps shot down. As it turned out – perhaps fortunately for the RAF – the Chinook did not arrive that night, but without radio contact, McNab could not possibly have known this at the time.

The decision to make for Syria is also questionable for two other reasons. First, although Ryan said that they had no written escape and evasion plan, Peter Ratcliffe, the Regimental Sergeant Major at the time, has stated for the record that there *was* such a written plan, and that it was filed with the Operations Officer at the FOB, al-Jauf. The plan, devised by McNab himself, was that, on compromise, Bravo Two Zero would head south for Saudi Arabia. Though Ryan admits that to head back to Saudi was the Regiment's official policy, he suggests, as does McNab, that the patrol had decided to make for Syria before they even left base. Moreover, their attitude to the escape and evasion plan, like the question of sleeping-bags, demonstrates a sad underestimation of the problems of the desert. Ryan says that he had considered packing a pair of shorts, because, talking the matter over at the FOB, they had decided that, walking and jogging, they could make the Syrian border in two nights. Such a plan made no provision whatsoever for the inevitable water-loss that such exertion would

bring. A man walking in the desert will require at least five litres of water a day in the cold season to maintain homeostasis. Running, he would obviously require much more – perhaps ten litres. For two days, each man would need twenty litres, weighing twenty kilos, plus his weapon, ammunition and other necessities, adding up to a minimum of a further twenty kilos. Running with forty kilos would require even more water, because of the extra exertion, and so the weight would keep spiralling upwards, and the speed of march down. It is this equation which makes travelling long distances on foot in the desert such a hazard.

If the patrol had decided to change the E and E plan at al-Jauf, why didn't they tell someone? Ryan and McNab indicate that they did mention it to one of the intelligence staff, but there was no guarantee that the man would even be present when they had to instigate it. In normal circumstances, it would have been perfectly acceptable to adjust the written plan, even on the ground, but this was a highly dubious strategy for a patrol that was out of contact with its base and had no means of informing it of the change. Though Coburn has accused the SAS command of betraying the patrol by failing to send in a rescue mission, in fact two helicopters – one British and one American – did fly in and search the area on the night of 26 January. By that time, of course, the patrol was on its way to Syria and out of the area specified on its own written escape and evasion plan: there was no way the heli pilots could have known that the plan had been changed. In heading for Syria instead of Saudi Arabia, as Ratcliffe has commented, 'McNab disobeyed his own orders.'

The second dubious aspect of the plan to go for Syria lay in its practicability. The route the patrol eventually chose – north towards

the Euphrates Valley, then due west towards the Syrian border – was certain to take them into highly populated regions. In the Middle East, river valleys are always densely inhabited, and likely to be the sites of industry, military defences and high concentrations of troops. The chances of an eight-man patrol slipping intact through those areas were not good. Saudi Arabia was further, but the way there was all sparsely inhabited desert, and the very fact that the Chinook on which they had infiltrated had made it in unscathed suggested that the area to the south was clear. Why, again, the decision to go for Syria, when all the odds appeared stacked against them in that direction?

ACCORDING TO THE DRAWN-TO-SCALE sketch-map in McNab's book, the first leg of the escape and evasion route took the patrol twenty kilometres due south, though in the text, McNab says it was 25 kilometres. Abbas and Hayil had told me that the team had run off to the south-west, and Ryan's map shows a squiggle going first a few kilometres south-east, then south-west, then due west, and finally north. What both Ryan and McNab do agree on is that their objective was to circle back to the road on which Abbas's house was situated and then head north into the desert beyond in an attempt to put their pursuers off their trail. With such conflicting accounts to contend with, I knew I could not hope to find the exact route the patrol had followed, but I could certainly get an idea of the country by walking due south.

My first day's walk almost turned into a disaster. From Ryan's and McNab's accounts, I had got the impression that the landscape south of the road was uniformly flat; it was, in fact, extremely rugged,

with rocky spurs and whaleback ridges cutting across it from west and east. This was the same area McNab said they had crossed going north on the night of 22/23 January, carrying 95 kilos per man, and which the blurb of his book describes as 'flat desert'. The going underfoot was difficult, the surface a rubble of polished limest one pebble-dash with beds of bristling desert grasses and occasional soft beds of pillow-sand thick with tamarisk and brilliant scarlet desert roses.

After several kilometres the land dipped into a wide, sandy gulch: the dried bed of the great Wadi Hawran, whose banks were lined with strips of wheat Abbas's family had planted. I understood now why Abbas needed his bulldozers. It was immensely hot, with a baking wind blowing in my face – conditions very different from the ones Bravo Two Zero had endured. I was dressed in a military-style shamagh, an SAS smock of 1942 vintage – a genuine antique with Bakelite buttons – track suit bottoms and desert boots. I was also wearing an escape-belt of the type the patrol would have carried, with water-bottles, dry rations, a bivvy-bag, map, compass and GPS, and a walkie-talkie to keep in touch with the vehicles carrying the crew and the Iraqi minders, who were supposed to remain within a kilometre of me.

I crossed the wadi and struggled up into the hilly country beyond and had already covered about twelve kilometres from the LUP when things started to go wrong. Squatting by a red-hot cairn of stones for a drink and a piece of pre-cooked flapjack, I received a message from my associate, Nigel Morris, who was with the convoy, saying that the GMC vehicles were unable to crossed the wadi and, in fact, had got stuck in the sand. Nigel told me that only the lighter pick-up belonging to the military escort could get across, and suggested

sending it to fetch me. I cursed the GMCs, which I had never trusted as real rough-country vehicles, and told him not to bother. I was just about to add that I would make for his position when the walkie-talkie went dead. Suddenly, without warning, I was experiencing precisely the same problem that Bravo Two Zero had experienced: I was totally cut off from my support in the desert. I had told Nigel not to send the military escort vehicle, but had not been able to say that I was heading back to the convoy. Now I was stuck. If the vehicle did not come as I'd instructed, I would be separated from the convoy. If I returned, I had no assurance that they would still be there.

I decided to go back, and by the time I had trudged the three kilometres up hill and down dale in the dehydrating wind, my water was down to a few mouthfuls. When I arrived back at the place where I had last seen the vehicles, there was nobody there. This was a blow. My water would soon be finished and I knew that in temperatures like these – mid-forties Celsius – a human being without water would be fried to a crisp in twenty-four hours. I was in no immediate danger because I could have walked the nine kilometres back to Abbas's farm, but I was certain the vehicles had gone on south-west, proba-bly looking for an easier way across the wadi.

After few moments' rest I decided to return to the cairn from which I had made my last transmission. The blast furnace wind was in my face again, and I knew I had to conserve what little water I had. As I stumbled wearily up and down the ridges, it suddenly occurred to me that water must have played a vital role in the patrol's escape and evasion plan. Indeed, Ryan admits that their original plan of making a dash for Syria directly in running shorts had to be modified to one taking them north to the Euphrates and then west

along the river because they had dumped their jerrycans with their Bergens and now had only a few litres of water each. Though it was bitterly cold then, the patrol was moving very fast on foot and losing large quantities of moisture which had to be replaced. As McNab himself points out, once a body has lost five per cent of its weight through dehydration, it begins to seize up, and if the deficit is not made up at this point, death will quickly follow.

I did not find the vehicles, but I did see a shadow on the desert surface some kilometres away which looked like some kind of habitation. As the minutes ticked by and I moved closer, I realized that it was a nest of Bedouin tents, with a three-ton truck parked outside. By now my mouth was parched dry and full of mucus and I felt exhausted from moisture-loss; my feet were staggering and stumbling over the stones. The wind felt like a heavy overcoat on my back, a weight pressing down on me, and my breath was evaporating like a vapour. I could almost feel the moisture being sucked from my pores. The tents were perhaps a kilometre away, but that felt like infinity in this stifling wind. I must have been about five hundred metres from the tents when a spectral white figure appeared. He held something shiny in his hand, and for a moment I feared it was a pistol. The Bedouin are hospitable people, but after what had happened near here ten years previously, you couldn't blame them for being on their guard. Even from that distance it must have been obvious that I was a stranger, dressed in quasi-military gear, and after all, this was still a country at war. I continued warily, and it was only as I got close that I realized the figure was a Bedouin boy and that what he was carrying was an aluminium bowl of water. With the hawk eyes of the Bedouin he must have perceived from more than a kilometre away that I was suffering from

thirst, and he had ventured out into the heat to meet me with this offering. The water was cool and clear – and was probably the best water I have tasted in my life.

After I had drunk, the boy led me to a tent where I was received graciously by an oldish man in a dishdasha and headcloth. Luckily, he had been at the feast at Abbas's place the previous night and recognized me. Within minutes he was offering me tea and coffee, and shortly after brought me a tray laden with goat's milk cheese, butter, ghee and flaps of unleavened bread. As I ate, I reflected on how welcoming the Bedouin were – probably the most welcoming people on earth.

One of the problems the SAS had in the desert was that they regarded it as a hostile environment. Even Peter Ratcliffe admitted that 'none of us felt completely at ease in the desert, for all our training, and for some of us years of experience'.[16] This unease was exacerbated by the fact that there were now few Arabic speakers in the Regiment, though back in Dhofar in the 1970s, there had been many who spoke the language fluently. Bravo Two Zero included not a single Arabic speaker, though even a limited knowledge of the language might have enabled them all to escape and might even have saved their lives. True, McNab's patrol had been compromised by Bedouin, but Abbas insisted that they had attacked the interlopers solely because they felt their home was under threat.

The SAS had discussed the problem of what to do about the Bedouin before being deployed in the desert, and some individuals had been in favour of killing or abducting any tribesman who saw them. In the event, this never happened, because there were enough moderate souls in the Regiment to realize that the tribesmen didn't have much interest in politics or war or who was fighting whom, as

long as they were left alone. A Bedouin's loyalty is always to his tribe, and though he may be forced to work for someone else, or do so for money, his employer will always be regarded as a foreigner, even if it is his own government. 'After a few chance encounters with the Bedou,' one sergeant of A Squadron wrote, 'they realized that the patrols were treating them a lot better than the Iraqis. To my knowledge they never compromised us – we were never followed up by Iraqis after meeting Bedou – they just let life go as it was. They stopped and chatted with us to pass the time of day. We'd give them tea, food and blankets, they'd give us information about where the Iraqis were and then they would leave. In the end, if there were Bedou about we actively let them know we were there rather than trying to hide.' [17]

Hiding like bandits in a wadi only six hundred metres from a house, Bravo Two Zero were certain to be seen as a threat, yet even then Abbas and his two companions had given them the benefit of the doubt by firing warning shots, following Bedouin custom. If the patrol had kept its cool and realized that those first two shots had not been aimed at them, or simply waved and made some answer in Arabic, they might have got away, or at least gained the advantage. As it was, their nerves drawn tight from the knowledge that they were alone and cut off in the fearful void of the Syrian Desert, they had overreacted, and in the end their own fear of the environment had defeated them.

After I had eaten and drunk tea, I explained my predicament to the old man and at once he offered to take me back to Abbas's farm in his truck. I accepted, even though I knew I could offer him nothing in return – to have offered money to a true Bedouin would have been a deadly insult. As we bounced and bumped back towards my

starting-off point, I decided that this must not happen again. I could find my way across the desert all right, but the vehicles would not be able to follow me without a guide who knew the area like the back of his hand. By the time we had arrived back at Abbas's place I knew I had already met the person I needed: the ideal guide would be Abbas bin Fadhil himself, the 'idiot on the digger' who had turned out to be anything but an idiot, the man who had compromised the Bravo Two Zero patrol.

# CHAPTER
# nine

AT THE FARM, ABBAS AND HIS brother welcomed me enthusiastically, ushered me into the guest hall and brought tea. They chortled when I told them of the misadventure. 'There are very few places where you can cross the Wadi Hawran with a car,' Abbas said. 'And you have to know where they are. Only the Bedouin know. I wanted to tell you that yesterday and to offer to be your rafiq, but you seemed so set on doing things your own way that I didn't say anything.'

I nodded, realizing that I had been so determined not to be deflected that I had forgotten the Bedouin tradition of taking a rafiq or companion from the local tribe when crossing their territory. The office of rafiq was almost sacred to the Bedouin. He acted not only as a guide, but also as a sort of ambassador from the local tribe, franking the foreign party across its neighbourhood. Once he had 'eaten

bread and salt' with his travelling companions, he would be obliged to defend them to the death, even against his own people, and to steal from them or injure them in any way was considered bowqa or treachery – the worst crime in the book as far as nomads were concerned. If a man couldn't be trusted as a rafiq, he was worthless and would soon find himself being avoided by his relatives. In a Bedouin tribe, no one actually had the authority to 'expel' a tribesman, but people would simply stop cooperating with him, which meant that he was on his own. Traditionally, to be 'on your own' in the desert was a death-sentence, because it meant that blood enemies could bump you off without fear of revenge.

I acknowledged my fault and asked Abbas if he would consider acting as guide and rafiq for the convoy in his own vehicle. He accepted enthusiastically. 'I think you should wait here for a couple of hours,' he said. 'If they don't return we'll take my pick-up and go to look for them. There's no chance we'll lose them. I know the country here blindfold – I was brought up here. My brother and I know all the country as far as Damascus in the north, Amman in the west and Kuwait in the south. You get to learn a lot when you travel by camel, and that's what we did when we were boys. We used to smuggle sheep across the borders. In those days, if you were a Bedouin no one asked you what country you belonged to, because the Bedouin had no country. The Anazeh – our tribal confederation – used to move their herds right from Syria down to Saudi Arabia at different times of the year. It's different now, of course.'

While we waited, I went over Abbas's account of the Bravo Two Zero story once again with him and Hayil, but the details did not alter.

'What's the matter?' Abbas enquired at one stage. 'Don't you believe us?'

'It's not that,' I said. 'But I have to be sure. Are you certain that there were no Iraqi soldiers involved?'

Abbas pointed solemnly at the ceiling. 'As God is my witness,' he said. 'Bedouin do not lie. It is the greatest of all sins. Why, even when I met the President himself I told him the truth.'

I was startled. 'What?' I said. 'You mean you met Saddam Hussein?'

'Yes.' Abbas said. 'It was while the war was on. He heard about our story – how we had spotted the commandos and taken them on alone, and he wanted to hear it from us and to reward us. We met him in Baghdad and he was very polite and friendly. There were two other people there: a man called al-Haj Abdallah from Ani, who belongs to the same tribe as I do, and who was involved in capturing one of the commandos, and another called Adnan Badawi, a Christian from Mosul, who had been hijacked by them.'

I gasped. Adnan Badawi was the same man who had told his story of being hijacked by British commandos to an Iraqi newspaper – I had the very article in my bag. This revelation opened up an entirely new can of worms, though. I had left Baghdad thinking no one had ever heard of Bravo Two Zero, and now I was learning that its defeat had been celebrated by Saddam himself. 'What did he give you?' I asked.

'He didn't give me anything personally, because he considered my father the head of the family. He gave him a Toyota pick-up – a brand-new one.'

'Good grief.' As I thought about it, I realized that Abbas's admission did alter the picture significantly. It meant that he had been

celebrated as a hero in his own country, just as McNab and Ryan had in theirs. It gave them a motive for exaggerating what they had done. On the other hand, I reasoned, it also tended to confirm their story. Why should Saddam have rewarded them if the major part in the drama had been played by the Iraqi army?

'What did you mean,' I asked, 'when you said that you told Saddam the truth?'

Abbas shrugged. 'He asked me why I did it, expecting me to say that I did it for the country. I told him that I did it because those men were threatening my home and family. Like I said, it is wrong to tell a lie.'


THE CONVOY TURNED UP LATER that afternoon, and Abu Omar was so furious that I had got separated from the vehicles for several hours that he insisted that we all returned to Baghdad. He was, he said, not happy with the conditions he had to work under anyway – he didn't like the food, couldn't sleep at night, and had not been able to have a shower in the past two days. He hadn't brought with him so much as a blanket or a water-bottle, and I wondered what kind of army officer would venture into the desert so unprepared. After a blazing row in Arabic, during which both of us probably said things we regretted later, the rotund Ali came to my aid and smoothed it over. To my surprise, he told me that he was the senior of the two minders and took priority over Abu Omar, so was perfectly within his rights to overrule him. Abu Omar, he informed me expansively, was only here to make sure we did not film where we were not allowed to. He did tell me that I should not have engaged Abbas as a guide without consulting him first, but in view of the

problems of the day he thought it was, generally speaking, a good move, and would let it ride.

The following morning, with Abbas now leading the convoy in his Toyota pick-up, I set off on foot from the Bedouin tent I had arrived at the previous day. It was still hot, but the wind had dropped and the going evened out into a flat, stony plain, melting at the horizon into a radiant sky. There were the tents of Bedouin families like dark stains on the landscape and, in places, thousands of black dots that were their flocks of sheep. Now the rough country was behind us, the terrain was ideal for four-wheel-drive vehicles, and I wondered again why McNab and his team had elected to go without them on this operation.

Ryan points out that B Squadron, being the reserve unit, had no proper desert vehicles like the Land Rover One-Tens or 'Pinkies' which A and D Squadrons had brought with them from Britain. The only vehicles available were what they derisively called 'Dinkies': short-wheel-base Land Rover 90s without weapon-mountings. They had tried these vehicles out in their training ground in Oman and pronounced them 'crap' – it was impossible to fire a general purpose machine-gun (GPMG) from them, and since there were no safety-belts, when put into a racing reverse, the passengers would be thrown out. Stan himself had been flung out and narrowly escaped being badly injured on a training run in Oman. Ryan admits that the team were alarmed at the idea of having to use these vehicles behind enemy lines. Of course, they would have been better than nothing. The main problem was striking a balance between escape and compromise. 'The most important reason for taking a Land Rover,' Peter Ratcliffe wrote, 'is that it provides a rapid means of escape from a contact, and the chance to return to the objective at a later date. Retreating

on foot with full kit is never fast, or easy. And that means that in a situation where your patrol is threatened, the only way out is to ditch most of the gear and run . . . Even if you managed to get clear, however, there is no way you can ever make another attempt to fulfil the mission . . .' [18]

If Abbas's claim that no Iraqi military pursued the patrol was correct, they could quite easily have reached a vehicle cache on the night of 24 January and beat a retreat to the border. The Iraqi air force was laying low anyway, and they were unlikely to have been hit from the air. Even at thirty kilometres per hour (twenty mph), the patrol could have made Saudi Arabia by vehicle in a day's hard drive. They would also have been able to carry the cold-weather equipment and supplies they needed more than anything in the Arctic temperatures, and enough heavy weaponry – Milan missiles, Browning machine-guns, mortars – to give a good account of themselves if things went noisy.

McNab writes that the vehicles would have stuck out like sore thumbs, or 'like balls on a bulldog', as he puts it, yet the country around the MSR was very broken, as I had discovered, full of wadis and re-entrants, and didn't flatten out for at least twelve kilometres to the south. There would have been plenty of places in which to conceal Land Rovers in that area. McNab, of course, did not know this before the mission, and had judged the ground from satellite pictures, which showed height but not depressions. 'Once you're on the ground,' Peter Ratcliffe wrote, 'you can usually find depressions to hide the vehicle in.'[19] This was certainly the experience of the Long Range Desert Group, which in 1942 had carried out vehicle-supported OPs in North Africa in country as stark and featureless as the Syrian Desert, and had never been compromised. SAS founder David

Stirling had realized that foot patrols wouldn't work in the desert the hard way, when, on the Regiment's very first operation, things had gone badly awry and two-thirds of a squadron, dropped in the desert by parachute, had died of thirst. As both Lawrence and Stirling knew, and as I had personally learned years ago, mobility is essential in the desert, where anything that stands still, dies. The distances involved are too vast for human legs alone: in summer or winter, in heat or cold, a man in the desert on foot unsupported has virtually no chance.

The Commanding Officer of 22 SAS had probably realized this when, on 21 January, the day before the mission, he tried to persuade the patrol to take Land Rovers. Peter Ratcliffe, who encountered the CO that day 'mad as hell' after his abortive discussion with Bravo Two Zero, felt that McNab was playing silly buggers. Asked by his boss to go and knock some sense into him, the RSM suggested strongly that McNab should take the colonel's advice. 'If it comes to a firefight, (motor vehicles) could well save your arse,' he told him. 'So . . . don't be a fool.' Ratcliffe noted that the rest of the patrol, including Ryan, seemed to support the decision. It was a course, the former RSM wrote, which he could not comprehend, but could do little to change. Although he outranked McNab and could theoretically have ordered him to take the vehicles, in SAS tradition, patrol commanders make their own decisions as to how they will go about their task, since they have to live with those decisions on the ground.

'I believed then – and I still do,' Ratcliffe wrote, 'that most, if not all, of Bravo Two Zero's misfortunes resulted from "McNab's" refusal to take advice before he even left base.' He was incensed that McNab made no reference to the advice given to him by the CO and

Ratcliffe himself before the mission in his book *Bravo Two Zero*. 'Considering what were, I'm convinced, the results of not following our advice,' Ratcliffe wrote, 'I find it odd that he didn't feel the meetings worth mentioning. After all, the failure of that mission ultimately cost the lives of three men, and led to four others being captured and tortured. That's a casualty rate of nearly ninety per cent.'[20]

It might be worth adding that while another B Squadron patrol, Bravo Three Zero, also declined to take a vehicle, the patrol commander aborted the mission immediately on seeing the terrain. The only B Squadron patrol to take a Land Rover, Bravo One Niner, was indeed compromised, but, thanks to its vehicles, managed to escape.

THE ONLY THING THAT SLOWED my progress was the hospitality of the Bedouin whose camps lay in my path. If I passed within three hundred metres of a tent, a dog would bark and soon a dark-swathed figure would appear and insist that I come in to drink tea. Traditionally, Bedouin are very prickly about hospitality and to pass a tent without stopping is considered an insult. Although it would be unheard of for a Bedouin to offer violence to someone who refuses his entreaties, his last resort would be the threat 'alayya at-talaq' – 'I will divorce my wife', which obliges him to do so if his hospitality is further refused.

I was stopped three times that morning and each time followed the same pattern. I would shake hands with my hosts and be ushered into the main part of the tent, where a fire of woody roots would be coaxed to life in the centre of the floor. While the kettle or coffee-pan went on the fire, more Bedouin would arrive as if by magic, and I would rise to greet each of them. When they had sat down

103

and the tea was being passed around, they would ask for what they called 'the news'. Bedouin are immensely curious about anything that goes on around them, and so avid for 'the news' that in the past they would ride hundreds of miles by camel to get it. The most important news is not politics or war, but the state of grazing and water, which is crucial to their survival. 'The news' also includes everything they have experienced over the past few days, and many nomads, being illiterate, have photographic memories and can describe what they have seen in incredible detail. Often in my journeys in the desert I have arrived at Bedouin camps to find that the people there know all about me already – the Bedouin grapevine, coupled with powers of observation honed sharp by years of experience in a landscape where nothing is hidden, is extraordinarily efficient. The tribesmen would have been happy to sit jawing over the news all day, but I had a walk to do and I was often obliged to refuse offers of vast meals and slaughtered sheep to escape. As I made my way south, though, the tents grew fewer. Often I came upon squares of stones around neat black rectangles of earth where tents had stood recently and I reflected once again that while this place seemed a wilderness to me, every square metre of it had been a home to the Bedouin at some time. By sunset that evening I had reached the place marked on McNab's map as the helicopter drop off point, exactly 20 kilometres due south of the LUP. The plain here was almost chillingly flat, and I could understand why the patrol had been moving so fast that night. To be caught out here in the open at first light could have been a sentence of death.

This was the place in which – according to McNab – the team had originally been dropped on 22 January and had lain down in all-round defence, acclimatizing to the night, as the noise of the

chopper's motors drifted slowly away. McNab says that he heard dogs barking and spotted a plantation within 1500 metres to the east, complete with water-tower, outbuildings and a house – uncannily like Abbas's place, which lay exactly 20 kilometres due north. I stood on the spot indicated by my Magellan and looked east. There was nothing there – no farm buildings, no water-tower, no plantation. This was remote, uninhabited country, far from roads. There never had been a house here, Abbas said, but I decided to check anyway, and a sweep to the east revealed nothing but the same rocky, flat, stubble-covered desert – no ruins, no debris, nothing. If there ever had been a building here as McNab writes, it had vanished without trace.

McNab says that they passed this point by about five kilometres on the night of the 24th, retreating from the firefight, though why he didn't wait for the heli due in at 0400 the next morning he doesn't make clear. Though he and Ryan differ on the actual distances they covered that night, both agree that they headed roughly south then west then north in a loop back to the road. At this point it became obvious that although none of the patrol had been hit in the ambush, there were two casualties – 'Stan' – who was suffering from extreme dehydration, and was in a state of near collapse, and Vince Phillips, who, according to McNab, had suffered some kind of leg injury while skirmishing out of the firefight. McNab notes that it was so completely out of character for Phillips to complain that his swollen leg must have been agony, while Ryan makes no mention of the injury at all.

Realizing that they had to move at the speed of the slowest, McNab changed the order of march, posting Ryan as lead scout with Stan after him, then Phillips, then McNab himself, and the other

four behind. If this is true, it is curious because Ryan maintains that he had insisted on being lead scout from the moment they had left the LUP, and that immediately after the firefight Vince Phillips was behind him as Number Two. Lead scout is the most risky position in a patrol formation, because at point he is the most likely to get bumped in a contact. If such a contact happens, numbers two and three in the line go to ground and cover the scout, who moves back tactically while the others go to ground. Ryan, however, says that Phillips kept falling back 'as if he didn't want to be near me' – clearly suggesting that the sergeant was afraid of getting hit in a contact. He also maintains that Phillips kept stopping and insisting that if they got bumped they should put up their hands and surrender rather than shooting back, or they would all be massacred. This is an unashamed accusation of cowardice against Phillips on Ryan's part, yet its veracity depends purely on the assertion that Phillips was Number Two in the line of march – otherwise it does not make sense. If McNab is right, though, and Ryan was not put in the lead until after the party had turned north many hours later, Ryan's accusation must be specious. The idea that Ryan was not lead scout from the beginning is suggested by Abbas's evidence that it was the seventh man, not the first, who waved.

Somewhere in the dark wasteland south of the road, McNab heard jets approaching from the north and halted to contact them on his TACBE. According to his account, he put his hand on Phillips's shoulder and told him the patrol was going to stop. Phillips acknowledged this, and assuming he would pass the message on, McNab halted and pulled the pin on the beacon just as the last two jets were going over. As McNab gave out his call sign and prepared to give a fix from the Magellan, he heard an American accented voice

drifting back across the airwaves reiterating the call-sign and asking him to repeat the message. However, by the time he had done so the jets were out of range. To his dismay, McNab then realised that the three men in front were no longer with him. He concluded that Phillips – in his 'numbed' condition – had not passed the message along the line. Now he had lost three men.

To be fair to McNab, he admits that though it was Phillips's responsibility to pass the message down to Stan and Ryan, as patrol commander he was 'a complete knobber' not to have checked. Ryan, who said later that he had never heard the jets, was stalking on fast ahead, did not realize the patrol had split until he reached the road, and was about to climb the ridge on the far side. Turning to confer with the patrol commander, he suddenly discovered that McNab was no longer with them. It was not long after midnight, and at least an hour since Ryan had last seen him – in that time the patrol had covered a lot of ground. When Ryan asked Phillips where the others were, he replied that he didn't know, and that they had 'just split off somewhere.' According to McNab, though, Stan later said that both he and Ryan had heard the jets and that Phillips had 'babbled' about 'aircraft and TACBEs' – suggesting that he had understood McNab's message that the patrol was going to stop. Ryan, however, does not blame Phillips for the split, admitting that he was on the verge of panic himself. More than anything, he was angry that he had got 'stuck' with the two 'casualties', one of whom (Stan) was 'out of the game' and the other (Phillips) 'didn't want to be in it'. The main firepower of the team was with McNab's group – since Stan had handed over his Minimi to McNab, the three of them now had between them only two M16s and a pistol. The Magellan had also gone with Mark. After sweeping the area with the kite-sight and

107

seeing nothing, Ryan attempted to call McNab on his TACBE with no result. Then, assuming command of his small squad – although Phillips outranked him – he decided that they ought to press on across the high plateau north of the road.

Was Phillips really to blame for the split as McNab obliquely suggests? Of course, it was a very dark night, with a freezing wind that forced the men to keep their heads down, low cloud cover, and poor visibility. The patrol had covered a long distance very fast and were exhausted and under extreme tension. In such circumstances, added to the fact that Phillips was in agony from his swollen leg, it would not be surprising if mistakes had been made. But it is notable that Ryan himself does not quote Phillips as saying McNab had halted to use the TACBE. It could, of course, be that McNab's message had *not* penetrated Phillips's 'numbed brain' as McNab says, but Phillips is dead and cannot speak for himself. Air force jets move pretty swiftly and the patrol was presumably well spaced out. Perhaps McNab was so anxious to contact the jets on hearing them that he failed to tell Phillips? According to Ryan's story, he had told McNab a full seven kilometres south of the road that he intended to 'push as hard as he could' until they had crossed it, despite the fact that he knew Stan and Phillips were disabled. Of course, even if he had not heard the shout, Phillips should have checked that McNab was behind him, but even if McNab's description is correct, the split need not have been a disaster had the patrol followed SAS standing procedure.

As an SAS patrol moves, the patrol leader should constantly be designating emergency rendezvous (ERVs) to which the patrol would return in the event of a problem – particularly a contact. This process is a basic SOP which every SAS recruit learns during selection, and

McNab even outlines the system in his book. Theoretically, when Ryan realized that the patrol had split, he should have led his section of it back to the nearest ERV and waited for the others to come in. Ryan says that while moving on from the TACBE contact, McNab's patrol spotted three men walking across their front, but assumed it was an Iraqi patrol and did not challenge them. Even if the SAS were being pursued by 'Iraqi patrols', which Abbas and his brother both denied, it seems highly unlikely that they would have been out on foot in threes. If they were not hallucinations, these three men were almost certainly the missing patrol members, but why, in that case, they should have been moving across the line of march must remain a puzzle. In any case, although the situation obviously demanded it, it is clear that McNab had not given out any emergency RV to the patrol. Whether Phillips did or did not pass the message along, therefore, is largely immaterial.

# CHAPTER
## ten

THAT NIGHT I CAMPED NEAR the crew and the minders at McNab's stated drop-off point. The evening was a hot one, the moonlight bright, and after dark the grasses were crawling with scorpions and spiders – more than I had ever seen anywhere at one time. These creatures only emerge from under their stones when the heat there becomes unbearable, and were not a problem for Bravo Two Zero in the freezing desert winter. Most scorpions inject a local toxin which causes a painful swelling, but a few carry a nerve toxin as powerful as a cobra's that can kill a man in four hours. To pass the time, Abbas organized a shooting competition among the military escort, using a plastic bottle at 100 paces. The only one who hit it consistently was Abbas himself.

In the morning I marched a brisk ten kilometres across an unrelenting plain, and then turned north once again until my way was

barred by a deep descent of hundreds of metres into a rocky valley. Almost certainly, this was where Bravo Two Zero had turned north, the route directed more by the landscape than time and distance. Here in the valley, among more broken country, there were ridges, dips and gullies that would give them more cover should the sunrise overtake them here. There was also no way vehicles could descend the steep cliffs, which would have thrown off any possible pursuers; Abbas had to take our convoy round by a circuitous route. It was even hotter down in the valley, and I struggled across a rubble of boulders and sat down for a snack and a mug of water in a sandy wadi, slowly frying. As I continued north, every hour or so I would see Abbas's pick-up bobbing out of the desert, keeping tabs on my progress.

Somewhere between here and the road to the north, Bravo Two Zero had split on the night of 24 January. Because of the time and distance discrepancies in McNab's and Ryan's accounts, it was impossible to know exactly where, but I was to get a clue from a totally unexpected source. About three kilometres south of the road, Abbas appeared once more and stopped me. He pointed out a mound on the side of a horseshoe-shaped ridge, where there appeared to be a small cairn of stones. Taking his AK47 with him, he led me up to the mound, which formed a kind of flat-bedded platform on the side of the ridge, facing south and at least ten square metres in area. If the wind had been from the north, this place, though high up, would have been fairly well sheltered on three sides. 'A few days after our gun-battle with the commandos,' Abbas said, 'the police found a weapon here. I only arrived later and I didn't get a good look at it, but I think it was a machine-gun. It was broken and couldn't be used, and we guessed it had been left here by the same people we had shot at back near the farm.'

I scratched my head. 'That's not possible,' I said. 'A British

patrol wouldn't abandon its weapons. It would be a disgrace.'

Abbas shrugged. 'I'm only telling you what they found,' he said. 'There were also signs that people had stopped here. The stones had been made into a kind of shelter and there were cigarette-ends and papers.'

This rang a bell, and I searched through my copy of McNab's book, looking for some reference. McNab notes that on the morning of 25 January, his section of the patrol decided to lie up on a lone knoll in an area of hard sand, on the top of which was a cairn surrounded by a dry-stone wall. I searched for a reference to an abandoned weapon and found none. I knew I had read it somewhere and I scoured Ryan's book too, without success. This was frustrating and I started to wonder if I had imagined it. Then it suddenly occurred to me that both books ended with retrospective accounts from the other members of the patrol, acquired when they were reunited in Britain after the mission. I turned to the back of *The One That Got Away* and found the page quickly. According to Ryan, McNab had told him that when they had established their LUP for 25 January, they had destroyed the radio's encrypting unit as well as their codebooks. They had also dismantled and scattered the parts of Stan's Minimi, which McNab had been carrying ever since Stan had gone down with heat exhaustion.

Suddenly it made sense. McNab had been hefting two weapons, and once Stan had disappeared with the others, there would have been no point in having his Minimi along, as no one but Rambo could fire more than one weapon at once. This was a key geographical clue, too, I realized. Since McNab would certainly not have abandoned Stan's weapon until after the split – and assuming it was Stan's weapon that had been found here – I knew I had now passed the place where the split had occurred.

The only nagging question was whether this could have been the patrol's LUP when McNab's sketch-map showed it as being at least 25 kilometres further on. If they had indeed spent the day of 25 January here, that meant they had covered no more than 45 kilometres the previous night – and that was going by the distances McNab gives in his text, which tally neither with his sketch-map, nor with Ryan's data. According to Ryan, the patrol marched only sixteen kilometres south, compared with McNab's 25, and only ten kilometres west, compared with McNab's fifteen. Ryan's map, however, indicates that the distances were even shorter. Allowing about another seven kilometres for the march north, this came to a total of only 34 kilometres (about 21 miles). Moreover, because of the doubt over McNab's story concerning the heli RV, I had been following Ryan's text to this point, and since I had found the place where the weapon had been abandoned near to my route, this suggested that Ryan's account was the more accurate.

The night had been pitch-dark, the conditions terrible, the going underfoot rocky and difficult, and at least as far as this point the patrol had been slowed down by two disabled men. They had been carrying weapons and belt-kit containing water, grenades and ammunition, weighing at least thirty kilos per man. They had stopped for some minutes, at first every hour, then every half hour, and had been further slowed down by the fact that the night-vision sight was ineffective due to lack of ambient light. If the contact had been at 1800 hours as all the information suggests, and they carried on until 0500 hours – the very latest cut-off point before first light – they had been going for a maximum of eleven hours at almost eight kilometres an hour. Anything over about six kilometres an hour is a running pace for most human beings, and Ryan says that the patrol were going

'as fast as possible without running'. A good marching pace for an SAS patrol in belt-kit is reckoned to be about five kilometres an hour, but this is in the best conditions, while the conditions Bravo Two Zero experienced that night were almost the worst possible.

I scanned the map again. From here to the second MSR was almost exactly fifty kilometres – precisely the distance McNab says they had covered to the metalled road the following night. If this had been the LUP for 25 January, then, the distance would tally on the second day, but would mean that what McNab said about covering 85 kilometres – "the distance of two marathons" – was wrong. Yet desperate men can sometimes achieve incredible things, and the patrol certainly had an incentive for moving fast. I had no reason to suspect Abbas of lying – after all, it had been difficult enough for me to find the reference to the abandoned weapon, which was not in the main part of the text. I had to admit, though, that this place bore little resemblance to the description of the 25 January LUP given in the book. There was no reason to suspect McNab was not correct over this. All in all, I thought, I should give McNab the benefit of the doubt – it was perfectly possible that Ryan had got it wrong and that they had broken up Stan's weapon long before they had reached the LUP on 25 January. This might have been a temporary LUP – a place where they had rested for half an hour or so before pressing on. In any case, whether it was 34 or 85 kilometres they covered that night does not detract from the true heroism they displayed: not the superhero ability to march vast distances on foot, but the incredible mental toughness they must have required not to give in to the desert at its most fearful, to keep driving forward right through the jaws of death.

In fact, the LUP of 25 January – wherever it was – almost proved

the undoing of them. They had found the place by 0500 hours, and by 0700 hours it was raining hard, to be followed in quick succession by sleet and snow. The last thing the SAS had expected was snow in the desert. It piled up over them in a drift as they lay behind the makeshift stone shelter, freezing their camouflage smocks solid and turning their shamaghs to cardboard. By 1100 hours the patrol was reduced to a shivering, quivering huddle of bodies, desperately trying to share their fading warmth. The human enemy was now forgotten; all thoughts were turned solely to survival. This was a time of great peril for Bravo Two Zero. All their lives hung in the balance, yet they managed to crack stupid jokes and exchange banter to keep their spirits up. It is to McNab's great credit that he realized the danger and decided to throw standard operating procedures to the wind, abandoning hard routine and lighting up a Hexamine stove, brewing up coffee and hot chocolate. Those brews probably saved the patrol's lives. By 1400 hours though, Coburn told McNab he was starting to go down with hypothermia. McNab asked him to hold on as long as he could, but within two hours everyone was slipping under, and though it was still daylight, McNab knew he couldn't risk remaining immobile any longer. By last light they would probably be unable to move at all, and by morning they would all be dead.

They moved out, shivering, staggering, mumbling to themselves, unable even to hold their weapons properly, trying to move fast enough to get the blood circulating and to generate some body heat. Though they managed to cross the metalled road they had been heading for that night, the trek was a terrible one – the worst conditions the SAS men had ever seen. It was pitch-black and desolate, with the north wind cutting into them like a blade, so chilling that they gradually started to switch off mentally and to become disoriented. Their

physical condition, McNab concluded, could not have been much worse. Recognizing the danger signals, and knowing the terrible wind-chill was eventually going to kill them anyway, McNab once again abandoned any semblance of tactical movement. He decided to backtrack to a sheltered wadi-bed south of the metalled road, where they huddled around Coburn, the worst affected and, again risking compromise, made brews of hot drinks and dished out food. They were on their feet again within two hours, but instead of marching north, back into the wind, they headed north-west along the wadi-bed, running parallel with the metalled road, which at least afforded a modicum of shelter and the possibility of protection from attack.

About midnight, Legs Lane – now lead scout – halted suddenly, and the others saw two armed men silhouetted on a hilltop. McNab wondered if they were two of the missing members of the patrol, but rejected the idea – no SAS man would have allowed himself to be skylined like that. Almost instinctively, McNab says, the patrol began to reach for their 'fighting knives', ready to deal with the men. They watched as the men inched up to within twenty metres of them, then suddenly jumped into the wadi and ambled away – 'The two luckiest men in Iraq,' McNab says.

McNab makes frequent reference throughout his book to these 'fighting knives' the patrol carried with them, which, he says, 'resembled the famous WWII commando dagger', even suggesting that the SAS men intended to use these daggers to take out the crews of the Scuds they were going to destroy. Although he himself spends half a page explaining how difficult it is to kill someone with a blade, he suggests that the use of such knives was commonplace in the Regiment. But as everyone who has served in the SAS knows, there is

no such thing as a 'fighting knife'. In World War II, some commandos and members of the Special Operations Executive – the SOE – were issued with stiletto-like commando knives for silent killing. They were not SAS soldiers. Fighting knives and unarmed combat may be part of the public myth of what Special Forces are about, but the reality is more prosaic. SAS men are issued with a clasp-knife – a multi-purpose tool like a Swiss Army Knife – and a bayonet. 'I have known a few SAS guys who carried slightly larger knives,' Peter Ratcliffe has written, 'but only for doing ordinary things – not for stabbing people or dogs or slitting sentries' throats.' [21]

Although McNab makes great play of what he calls 'jap-slapping' or unarmed combat in his autobiography, Ratcliffe points out that only the rudiments are taught in the SAS – principally for self-defence against other people armed with knives. The SAS themselves have developed a means of close-quarter battle (CQB) using pistols, which renders knife-fighting and jap-slapping obsolete. After all, not even a black belt can duck a 9mm bullet. As Ratcliffe has explained, 'If you have to kill someone or some animal, in combat, or otherwise, while on active service, then you use your rifle or pistol. There is no unit of the British Army which uses knives – other than bayonets – garrottes or cross-bows to dispose of the enemy. Any soldier who asks you to believe differently is either lying or has himself been taken in by some of the nonsense.' [22]

Before first light on 26 January the patrol lay up in a hollow, where they remained for the rest of the day. That afternoon they were compromised by a shepherd – a harmless, friendly old Bedouin who offered them milk, cheese and dates, and left them in peace. Once again, their lack of Arabic prevented them from gaining what might have been vital information from him. Having moved on a

little in case he informed anyone of their position, they halted again and took stock. They all knew now that the weather had become a more fearsome enemy than the Iraqis, and would kill them more quickly and efficiently if they pressed on into the devastating wind. Despite the cold, they were dehydrated, and they knew that water would soon become a serious problem. Although the Syrian border was only twelve hours' march away, McNab probably doubted that Bravo Two Zero could make it intact through another such night as the two they had already endured. On the other hand, there was a main road nearby, and by the sound of it, there were vehicles in plenty. Why not simply take one and make a last, desperate bid for freedom? It would be a risky gambit, but whatever happened, it would be better than freezing slowly to death in the desert. They decided that they would wait until dark, then hijack the first vehicle that came along the road from whatever direction. It was no doubt the right decision, but it was ultimately to sign the death warrants of two of McNab's group, and to consign the rest to weeks of torture and incarceration.

# CHAPTER
# eleven

FROM THE POINT WHERE THE patrol had split I had the option of following either McNab's or Ryan's route. Though I was still anxious to find out what had happened to Vince Phillips, I decided to go with McNab as far as the place where he and his team were captured or killed, then double back to the point of divergence and follow Ryan, Phillips and Stan.

I crossed the ragged, boulder-strewn country to the south of the road, working towards the granite ridge that marked the tableland where both Ryan's and McNab's groups had lain up on 25 January. The MSR itself came as something of a surprise. Both Ryan and McNab repeat the intelligence brief they had received before the operation, declaring that the road was a system of tracks amalgamated together, varying in width from two and a half kilometres to six hundred metres. I had followed the MSR as far as Abbas's

place already and had found no sign of this vast rural highway: up to that point, at least, it had been a narrow country road, asphalted in places. There was no sign on the map that it ever got any wider, and though it wasn't asphalted where I was now crossing, it seemed extremely unlikely that it had ever been more extensive than it was. Bounded on the northern side by the ridge, it could never have expanded far in that direction, and to the south it ran through flat fields of millions of boulders. Unless these boulders had appeared since 1991, it was inconceivable that the road had been wider in that direction either. Perhaps the MSR might be an amalgam of tracks further west, but here it was an ordinary country track, no more than five metres wide. I wondered where the intelligence report about the road had originated, and why McNab and Ryan had repeated it even though they had been on the ground and must have known the reality.

I crossed the MSR and climbed the ridge, finding myself on the stark plateau that lay between here and the second MSR to the north – the road McNab's party had reached by the evening of 26 January. The two roads did not run parallel, but formed sides of a triangle, meaning that the plateau was wider the further west you went. According to McNab's intelligence brief, the land did not drop more than fifty metres between here and the next road, and this at least looked accurate. In fact, the area was mind-bogglingly uniform, so stark and clean that it strained the senses. The occasional blemish on the surface looked grotesque and gigantic, drawing the eye towards it automatically, while close up it resolved into nothing more than a pebble or a tin can. Here, the Bedouin tents were fewer, and all day I walked on into a shimmering haze. Often I had the familiar feeling that I was not making progress at all,

just marking time on the same spot while the horizon remained equidistant before me, and the sky beat out a percussion of unforgiving heat. In such nothingness, even the small details on the surface become meaningful – the track of a lizard or a scorpion, the bones of a dead bird, fragments of rope fibre left behind by a shepherd, a circle of stones that was the only trace of a nomad camp. As time passed I began to make out strange shapes before me: humps of earth that stood out unnaturally, reflecting the light in unexpected colours. In the far distance there were pylons whose heads hovered on the skyline; occasionally I would spot a moving truck bloated by the distorting shimmer.

After about twenty kilometres the land began to furrow and break up a little, and I saw that the strange earthworks to my immediate front were in the centre of some sort of huge installation with a barbed wire fence running about five kilometres along its periphery. There were outbuildings and watch-towers, and my pace became warier until I realized that the fence was derelict and the place uninhabited and overgrown. It hit me very suddenly that this was an abandoned military installation of some importance and, consulting my map, I noticed that it was marked as a large sealed compound with a road leading to it. Close up, it was obvious that the place was not only abandoned, but totally wrecked. The ziggurats of earth I had seen from way back were the walls of craters, and there were masses of ruined masonry, including entire walls of stressed concrete that had been torn apart and hurled aside like a giant's building bricks. Evidently the installation had been of strategic importance – a command centre, a biological warfare plant, a Scud control centre, even a nuclear plant. Either it had been hit by wave after wave of Allied bombers during the war, or it had been demolished since

under UN supervision. It occurred to me suddenly that this must have been the place the anti-aircraft guns McNab saw had been guarding – at about fifteen kilometres from Abbas's house, it was also the place to which Abbas would have sent his messenger, which explained why it had taken the military so long to get back to the scene of the firefight. It might also account for the amount of military activity McNab says was evident in the area. The bombing runs that had come in over this region – even those that Abbas said had accidentally killed Bedouin and destroyed buildings nearby – had probably been intended for this place.

The installation was huge, and I wondered if that fact might substantiate McNab's statement (in an interview with the BBC in 2000) that there were more than three thousand Iraqi troops in the area: 'effectively two armoured brigades that shouldn't have been there, that intelligence hadn't picked up. They only discovered this four days after we arrived.'[23] Judging by the size of it, this compound could easily have contained three thousand troops, but McNab does not make reference to these two armoured brigades in his book. He recalls seeing armoured personnel carriers at various stages, but not the tanks one would expect to comprise an armoured unit (as opposed to a mechanized infantry unit). Since the compound is clearly marked on the map, Military Intelligence must have known it existed, and must also have been aware at least of the possibility of its being protected by large numbers of men. If they were there, though, I found no evidence that they contributed to Bravo Two Zero's compromise – the only evidence I had uncovered indicated that the patrol had been spotted and shot up by three civilians.

Leaving the installation on my right, I started to descend into a deep valley criss-crossed with stripes of yellow wheat. In the

distance the pylons suddenly came into clear focus, running across my front only a stone's throw from the road that ran north-west to the towns of Krabilah and al-Qaim on the Syrian border, and south-east to al-Haqlaniya. Somewhere along that road, I knew, McNab and his group had hijacked a car on the evening of 26 January 1991.

The plan had been for three of the group to hide in the ditch nearby, while McNab and Consiglio posed as Iraqi soldiers, one of whom was badly wounded. They would flag down a vehicle and, as soon as it stopped, the others would pile out with their weapons and heist the car. McNab and Consiglio were probably assigned the front job because they were both dark – McNab half Greek and Consiglio half Italian – and were more likely to be taken for Iraqis than the others.

At last light, the two of them stood on the roadside with some trepidation, knowing that this was the make-or-break gambit. As the sound of an engine came to their ears, heading from the direction of Krabilah, Consiglio lay in McNab's arms, groaning, playing the wounded soldier, while McNab began to flash his torch anxiously at the oncoming lights. The vehicle stopped and, to his amazement, McNab saw that they had halted a full-blown New York Yellow Cab, straight out of a 1950s movie, complete with chrome bumpers and white-walled tyres. As the driver and two passengers climbed out to help, they found themselves staring into the muzzles of automatic weapons produced by three desperadoes in camouflage who had just jumped out of the ditch. One of the passengers, McNab said, was so terrified that he produced a Madonna and whimpered that he was a Christian, pointing to the driver and repeating, 'Muslim! Muslim!' The driver himself was having hysterics,

screaming that the cab was his livelihood and that he couldn't survive without it. Ignoring the bickering, McNab and his team shoved the three Iraqis into the ditch and piled into the car, turning it back towards Krabilah. With McNab himself driving, they screeched off on what they hoped would be the last leg of their escape and evasion route.

It was warm in the cab, and luxurious after the conditions they had endured for the past few days, and for a moment they felt euphoric. But their triumph was short-lived. On the outskirts of Krabilah they ran into a permanent VCP (vehicle checkpoint), where Iraqi soldiers were checking the traffic. They stopped the car in the queue and waited tensely as a guard made his way up the line of vehicles. Suddenly the man pressed his face against the window on the left hand side and Legs Lane – in the front passenger seat – fired one round across McNab's body, shattering the glass and dropping the man instantly. The patrol then piled out of the taxi shooting blind towards the VCP as all hell broke loose. Civilian drivers threw themselves into the footwells of their vehicles while two more guards running for cover on the right were cut down in their tracks by bursts from the Minimis. The first men across the road put down covering fire until the others were across, then all five SAS men raced into the desert, followed by a hail of rounds from the VCP and a roar of engines and screaming voices. The entire contact, McNab reckoned, had taken all of thirty seconds.

That night I slept without my bivvy-bag on an exposed ridge similar to the one McNab describes, behind a cairn of stones, trying to at least get an idea of what it had been like for them. As an experiment it failed completely – it was so warm that I slept like a log.

The next morning there was exciting news. While I had been walking, Nigel Morris had been scouring the entire Anbar region trying to find the hijacked taxi-cab itself. This was not the needle in the haystack it had first looked like because we knew from the newspaper piece we'd been handed in Baghdad that the vehicle was a communal taxi registered as 'Anbar 73'. Since the number of such vehicles was obviously limited and since the police kept a record of them all, Nigel had been able to trace it to the town of Rumadi. After some brilliant detective work, he had actually discovered the cab in a garage in the town – on its last legs, he reported, but still running. He had had it sent to Krabilah on a lorry, and I later asked Abbas to go and pick it up. I also enquired if there was any news of Adnan Badawi, the man who had apparently been a passenger in the taxi when it had been hijacked, but Nigel told me the Ministry had been unable to reach him.

There was only a brief walk that morning, over undulating country, under the line of pylons and out to a high ridge overlooking the main road. As I stood there enjoying the view, a pick-up turned up with local officials, demanding to know what was going on. They were quickly soothed by Ali and our military escort. I descended to the road and walked along it until I had satisfied myself that I was at least within the rough area of the hijack. All I had to do now was to wait for Abbas and the taxi to arrive.

The road wasn't particularly busy, and few vehicles passed. In the early afternoon, though, I heard the grind of gears and saw a white saloon approaching me from the direction of Krabilah. I stood up as it came nearer and, slowing to a halt, I was astonished to see that Abbas was driving. 'What's this?' I demanded, after we'd greeted each other.

'This is the taxi that was hijacked,' Abbas said. 'The one Adnan was riding in. You asked me to bring it for you.'

I examined the vehicle carefully. It was not and clearly never had been a New York Yellow Cab. It was a common Toyota Crown, clearly a great deal more than ten years old, and in poor condition. There was a large crack in the front windscreen, but it looked as if it had been made by a stone rather than a bullet, and the window on the driver's side, which McNab said Legs had shot the soldier through, appeared both original and intact. There were no chrome bumpers or white-walled tyres, and no tassels or other decorations in the interior. Finally I checked the registration, which consisted of only two numbers – 73 – exactly as noted in the newspaper report.

'But this can't be it,' I said. 'This is a Toyota Crown, and the hijacked car was a yellow New York taxi.'

Abbas chuckled. 'There are no yellow taxis in Iraq,' he told me. 'There aren't even any yellow cars. Someone must have been joking with you.'

I wondered if the number-plate might have been changed, but Nigel later confirmed that this was the original car registered as 'Anbar 73', and told me that it had actually changed hands seven times since 1991. For that reason he had not been able to find the original driver, Ahmad al-Hitawi, and though Uday had managed to contact Adnan Badawi in Mosul, he had refused to talk to us. I didn't like the sound of this, as it suggested he might be covering something up, but I consoled myself with the fact that we had Abbas, who had heard the story from Adnan first-hand, and also the newspaper cutting.

I asked Abbas if he knew the exact spot where the hijacking had

*Above*, Michael, on the trail of Bravo Two Zero. 'When most people think of deserts, they imagine sand dunes rolling on endlessly like the waves of a sea, but the Syrian Desert is nothing like that: in fact, there is very little sand. It is more like desolate, arid moorland, rocky or muddy, with stunted hills and high plateaux, occasionally cut by steep-sided wadis.'

*Below*, The LUP (Lying-Up Position) where the Bravo Two Zero patrol was compromised. 'Given Bedouin powers of observation and the very proximity of the place, there had really been no more chance of the SAS escaping unseen than if a band of Iraqis had landed on a British council estate.'

Abbas bin Fadhil: 'Why, even when I met the President himself I told him the truth.'

OPPOSITE
*Above*, Abbas's family: 'He asked me why I did it, expecting me to say that I did it for the country. I told him that I did it because those men were threatening my home and family.'

The military escort contemplates his tea as more of the true story of Bravo Two Zero is revealed.

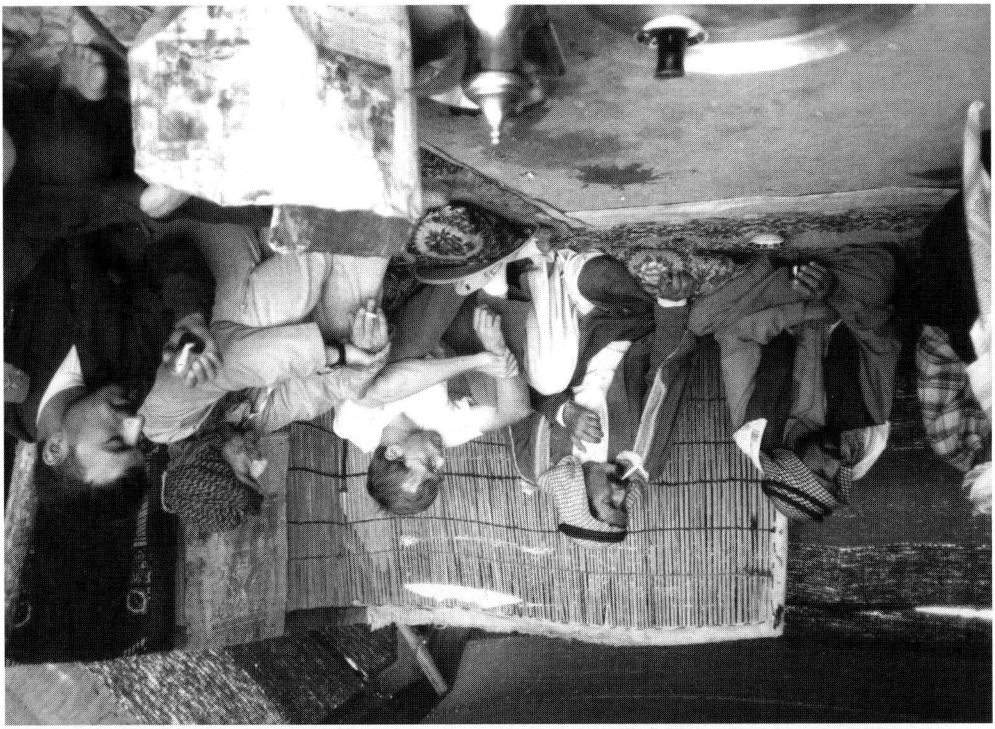

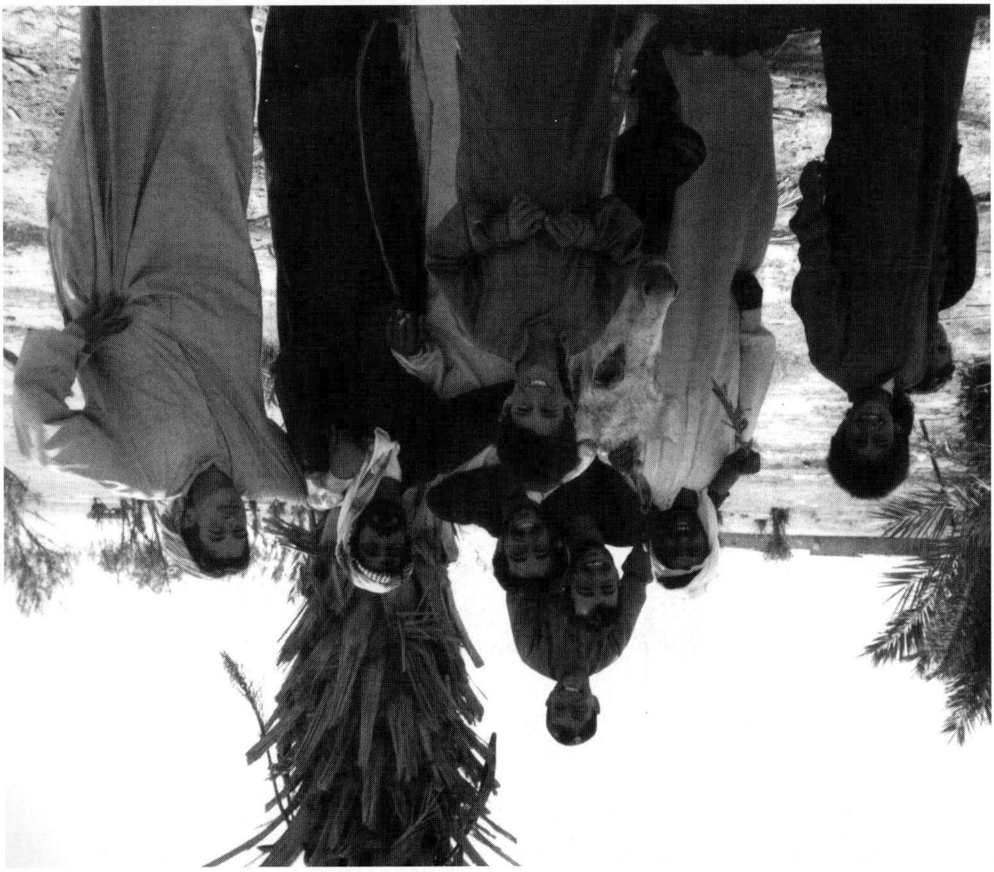

*Above*, the bulldozer from which Abbas spotted the patrol without the SAS realizing they had been compromised.

The taxi hijacked by Andy McNab: not a New York Yellow Cab, but an ageing Toyota. Significantly, the driver knew McNab's real name, something not revealed in *Bravo Two Zero*.

OPPOSITE
*Above, left to right* Hayil, Mohammed, Abbas, Michael and Adil (the shepherd-boy). Michael holds a clip of 5.56mm ammunition captured from the patrol.

The pump-house where Legs Lane was captured, by that time dying of hypothermia. Dinger was taken prisoner nearby.

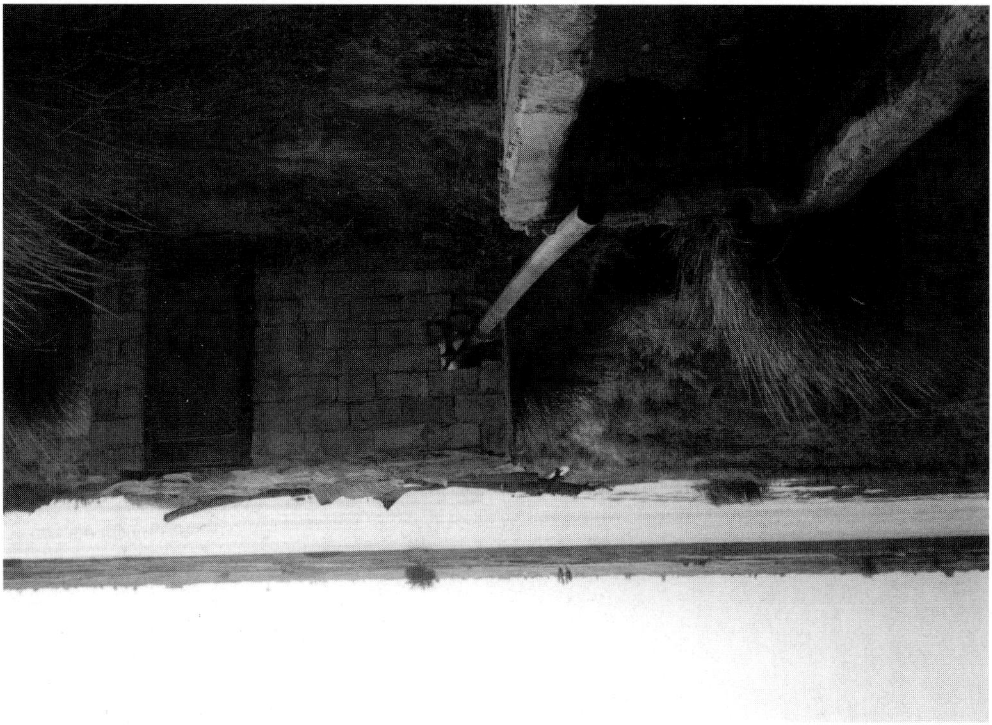

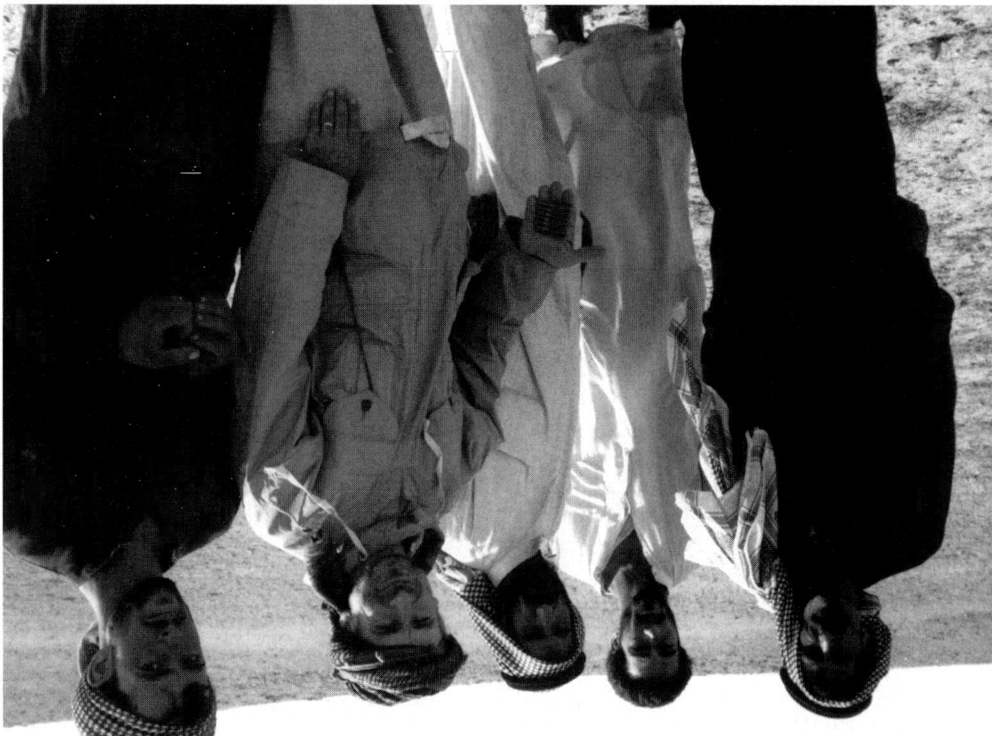

Michael with one of the Minimi 5.56mm machine-guns captured by the Iraqis from Bravo Two Zero. Belt-fed, they enabled the small patrol to put down a great deal of fire albeit for a short time.

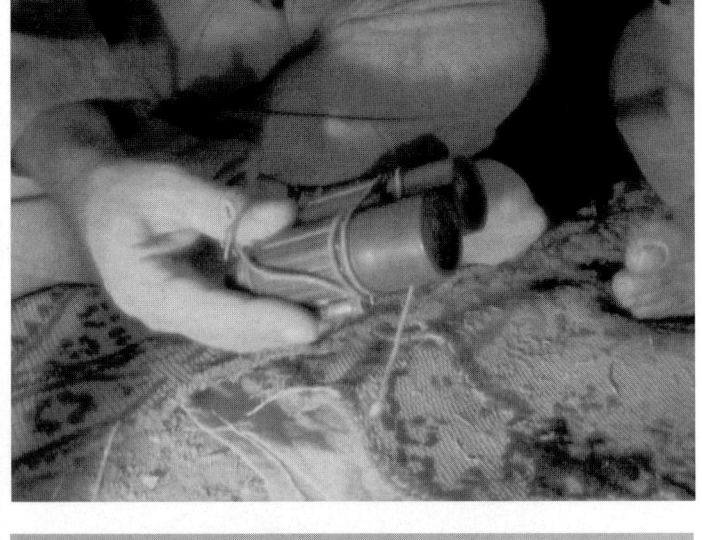

*Above*, the field where Coburn was captured by the Iraqis.

Vince's binoculars, bought in Abu Dhabi just prior to his last mission.

Where Andy McNab was captured: only one member of his patrol would succeed in escaping to Syria after the agreed plan to withdraw to Saudi Arabia was ignored.

*Left to right* Michael, Ahmad and Subhi the lawyer. Bob Consiglio was shot and killed here by armed civilians pursuing the remaining members of the patrol.

Michael and Mohammed stand by Vince's cairn.

taken place, and he told me that he had a very good idea. I got in the car beside him and, as he accelerated, I had to remind myself that this was the actual car McNab and the others had driven off in on that day ten years earlier, even if it wasn't a New York Yellow Cab as McNab had written. The place Abbas drove me to stood in a slight dip in the road, with a machine-made ditch on the northern side – the right-hand side looking towards Krabilah. Abbas confessed that he wasn't absolutely certain that this was the place – he knew the country here like the back of his hand, but was only going on what Adnan had told him ten years earlier. No matter; I was certain from my own map reading that we must be within a kilometre of the spot.

Abbas reminded me that we had passed some sort of industrial installation on our way. 'That was where Adnan was stationed,' he told me. 'He was a sergeant in the police, who were guarding that place. That night – 26 January – he was going to al-Haqlaniya to pick up the wages for his men. It was just before sunset, about five o'clock. He told me that he was walking along the road when this taxi came along – it was being driven by a man called Ahmad Hitawi who was taking his son, a soldier, back to his camp. Adnan flagged it down and got in, and before they'd gone very far they saw two men in camouflage uniforms by the side of the road. One was lying on the ground, he said, and the other was beckoning to them. Adnan thought they were Iraqis and that one of them was injured – it wouldn't have been surprising if you remember there were air attacks going on all over the country at that time. When they got out to see if they could help, the one lying down got up suddenly, and three others came out of hiding with weapons. Realizing they were enemy soldiers, he told them he was a Christian and talked to them in

English. They decided to take him with them, offering him gold to help them, and turned the car round. They just left the other two, and drove off towards Krabilah.'

I stopped him. There was a major discrepancy here with McNab's story. McNab was adamant that he had left all three Iraqis in the ditch and that the patrol had driven off on their own, whereas Abbas was telling me that they had taken Adnan with them. If this was true, then Adnan must have witnessed the firefight at the checkpoint outside Krabilah, when a number of Iraqis had been killed.

I asked Abbas about this, and he shook his head. 'He didn't mention anything about Iraqis being killed,' he told me. 'He said that they came to the checkpoint outside Krabilah, but he had already told them they would never get through, so they stopped the car before they got there and they all got out – five of them. They asked him to drive the car through the checkpoint without saying anything to the guards there, and to pick them up about three kilometres further on. Adnan said he pretended to go along with it and they were happy. As soon as they'd gone he drove to the checkpoint and denounced them to the police.'

'He didn't talk about the commandos having shot anyone at the checkpoint?'

'Definitely not. He said they left the car before they got near it'.

When I thought about it, this seemed a far more reasonable account than McNab's claim to have fought his way out of a checkpoint. After all, checkpoints exist to stop people doing just that, and they are likely to be bristling with gun-emplacements. A far more workable plan – and one more in keeping with SAS principles – would have been simply to leave the car before the VCP, as Abbas described, and disappear into the desert. Staying in the queue would

have made a firefight inevitable – there was no way five camouflaged men who hardly knew a word of Arabic between them were ever going to bluff their way through. But was this the truth? It all hinged on whether or not the patrol had really taken Adnan with them in the vehicle.

Later, turning to the newspaper interview with Adnan himself, I found that the basic facts tallied largely with what Abbas had reported. What possible reason, therefore, could he have in refusing to talk to us, I wondered? Did his silence indicate that this was all a set-up – that McNab was correct and that the story that he had been with them in the taxi was a lie? A careful second translation of the newspaper article suggested a possible motive. First of all, Adnan stated that the patrol had offered him a large sum of money, not to help them escape, but to guide them to Iraqi military units stationed in the desert, their objective being, he said, 'to discover the strength of our forces in the area'. He added that the patrol had wanted to kill the owner of the car and his son, but that he had saved their lives by declaring that he would refuse to cooperate with the commandos if they did so. Adnan also claimed that he had warned the SAS that they would not get through the checkpoint, and 'persuaded' them to get out of the car five hundred metres short of the VCP, telling them that he would pick them up three kilometres further on.

These additions seemed to me to be false. The idea that the exhausted, starving SAS team had demanded to be taken to see Iraqi military units when they were desperate to get away from them was ludicrous. And the upstanding Iraqi citizen who had saved the lives of his co-nationalists did not sound much like the man who, according to McNab, had screamed that he was a Christian to preserve his own life, and pointed out that the others were Muslims. If this is

true, then he had obviously been terrified by McNab and the others into helping them, and had sought to cover that up by portraying himself as a more active mover and shaker in the story. He had saved the country by diverting the enemy from their mission and tricking them at the VCP. It was pure speculation, of course, but I guessed that he had refused to cooperate with us because he feared we knew the truth.

This was a fascinating sideline, but Adnan's pretensions to heroism did not affect the question of whether he had been in the car with the SAS as far as the checkpoint, or if he had been left behind in the desert as McNab wrote. At the end of the article, though, came a clincher that erased any reasonable doubt: Adnan let drop that 'the leader's name was Steven'. Even if he had somehow managed to get hold of a copy of *Bravo Two Zero*, which was not available in Iraq, how, unless he had actually established some kind of rapport with McNab, could he possibly have known his real name?

Ryan corroborates both Adnan's story and my theory that his alleged heroism was a cover for his abject terror. Presumably quoting from what McNab or one of the others had told him after their return to Britain, Ryan writes that the patrol took one man with them in the car because he looked so terrified that they thought he might help them. He adds that they got out of the car before the checkpoint, having arranged that the Iraqi would pick them up further on, whereupon he promptly shopped them to the police.

# CHAPTER
# twelve

THE ROAD TO KRABILAH TOOK US through villages of breeze-block shanties standing among the debris of industrial society: goats and sheep nuzzled around discarded tyres, engine-blocks, hulks of vehicles and piles of non-biodegradable rubbish. There were run-down military camps: S60 guns without crews, armoured personnel carriers looking battered and immobile. Parked along the way were dozens of oil-tankers carrying consignments of crude to Jordan. On the outskirts of Krabilah we came to a desolate-looking concrete hut on the side of the road. The hut was abandoned and ruined, but it had obviously once been part of a vehicle checkpoint. 'This is it,' Abbas told me. 'This is the checkpoint Adnan talked about.'

I had found Bravo Two Zero's VCP, but without an eyewitness as to what had happened here on the night of 26 January 1991, it was nothing but an abandoned hut. Whatever had really taken place here,

I thought, this point had marked the beginning of the end for McNab's section of the patrol. For two of them – Consiglio and Lane – that taxi ride had been the last real journey of their lives. As we pulled away from the deserted hut and into the town I realized that I was sitting in the very seat that Legs Lane had sat in on that day.

Krabilah was a one-horse town, a settlement spread thinly along the road to Syria, where we checked into a hotel with rooms like ovens opening off walkways that looked down on an alley. Across the street was a spacious restaurant-cum-teashop where forlorn hunks of lamb hung in the window and an immensely fat youth with balloon biceps could be seen slicing meat for kebabs with a vast blade like a miniature scythe. The owner of the restaurant was a pale, haggard-looking man called al-Haj Nur ad-Din, an engineer who had once worked at a brick factory outside Krabilah that had been destroyed by Allied bombing raids. Though he complained bitterly about the loss of the factory, Nur ad-Din welcomed us with no less courtesy than the other Iraqis I'd met. Over tea and hookah-pipes, he told me that everyone knew the story of the British commandos who had been captured or died here in 1991. Krabilah was a small town – actually not much more than a village – and everything that went on here was common knowledge. It wasn't every day that such a thing happened.

I asked him if there was anyone still serving in the army here who had been here in 1991. 'It wasn't army business,' Nur ad-Din said. 'It was all dealt with by the police, and a lot of ordinary citizens were involved, too. There was an alert that foreign commandos were in the area long before they were found here.'

Nur ad-Din gave me the name of a police sergeant major who had been stationed in Krabilah since 1991, and the minders

obligingly traced him for me. He turned out to be as good an adver-
tisement for the Iraqi police as it would have been possible to find.
Ahmad was surprisingly young – a tall, slimly built, charming man
with film-star good looks – and not in the least grizzled or sergeant
major-like. He wore olive-green fatigues, without a cap, a weapon
or rank insignia – nothing but a pin bearing the face of Saddam Hussein on his chest. I wondered if it was some sort of medal. Ahmad
said he had been here in Krabilah on the night of 26 January 1991,
and had been involved in hunting the British commandos and capturing one of them.

'It started quite early in the evening,' he said. 'I was on duty at the
main police station in Krabilah town. A man arrived – a police sergeant who I think was a Christian from Mosul – and reported that
he had been kidnapped by a group of five British commandos, who
were heavily armed and carrying some sort of transmitter – a thing
like a tiny computer with a keyboard. He had tricked them, he told us,
by dropping them about half a kilometre from the checkpoint outside Krabilah and telling them he would pick them up three kilometres further on. He reported it to the police at the checkpoint, and
they sent him on to the police in Krabilah.'

I took out the newspaper cutting of the interview with Adnan
Badawi and showed Ahmad the head and shoulders portrait of
Adnan himself. 'Is that him?' I asked.

He squinted at it and nodded. 'It looks like him,' he said. 'But
don't forget it's ten years since then.'

I asked if the man who had reported the kidnapping had mentioned any shooting at the VCP. 'No,' Ahmad said. 'He never mentioned shooting at all. He said the commandos just left the car and
went off into the desert.'

'So there were no police deaths at the checkpoint that night?'

'Not at all. Nobody was killed or injured at the checkpoint. If they had been, I would have known, because I arrived there myself not long afterwards. Everyone was excited about the presence of the foreign commandos, but there definitely hadn't been any shooting at the VCP. The shooting came later.'

I asked Ahmad to look at the taxi we had brought from Rumadi, and he confirmed that it was the vehicle Adnan had arrived in that night. Then I asked if he would take me to see where the action had taken place. With Abbas driving again, we motored several kilometres back out of Krabilah down the road we'd come in on.

Ahmad stopped us at the same abandoned concrete hut Abbas had shown me on the way into town. 'This was the checkpoint,' Ahmad told me, 'and it was permanently manned in 1991, by quite a large contingent of police. I arrived here at around eight o'clock with seven other policemen to check out what the man who'd been kidnapped had told us, and I found everything completely okay – no one dead or injured. There was a lot of traffic on the road, and everyone was driving very fast because there were air-raids that night. The odd thing, though, was that on our way here we passed two men trying to stop cars on the opposite (south) side of the road. One man was lying on the ground, looking hurt, and the other was flashing a torch at the cars, but no one was stopping – everyone was driving on very fast. The man from Mosul was with me, and I said "Is that them?" and he said "Yes. That's just what they did when they caught me." Anyway, we decided not to approach them and drove past pretending we hadn't seen anything. I don't think they noticed us.'

McNab makes no mention in his book of this second attempt

to hijack a vehicle. He states that, having legged it into the desert, leaving behind them three Iraqi dead and a confusion of sporadic shooting, screams and revving engines, the patrol regrouped. None of them, McNab said, could actually believe they had survived. A quick fix on the Magellan told them they were only eleven kilometres from Syria and freedom. Judging by their previous speed, they should have been able to cover this in under ninety minutes. McNab knew that they had to make it that night, because there was little chance of the patrol being able to lay up safely here the following day.

They set off west at a jogging pace, soon entering an area of habitation where dogs barked and generators hummed. They were near enough to the road to see that it was already being patrolled by armoured personnel carriers, and suddenly the moon came out, making their light-coloured desert camouflage suits stand out like beacons. Suddenly, they were spotted. Three or four vehicles screeched to a halt and disgorged soldiers, who began blazing away at them. Anxious to conserve the little ammunition left to them, they ran for it, covering four hundred metres at breakneck speed. Coming over a crest, they saw the lights of Abu Kamal in Syria twinkling tantalizingly in the distance, so near and yet so far away. 'I could almost taste the place,' McNab wrote. As they cleared the crest they were highlighted and seen by an anti-aircraft battery, which opened up on them, and they switched north, sprinting across a road and into a built-up area that led down to the banks of the Euphrates.

I asked Ahmad if he could remember the place he had seen the SAS men, and he replied that it was easy, because it had been by a road-bridge about three kilometres from the VCP. We drove back towards the town until we came to a concrete bridge with iron

railings, where Ahmad told Abbas to stop and we jumped out. 'This is where they were when I first saw them,' Ahmad said, 'and they were still here when we got back. By that time we had managed to collect about seven vehicles at the checkpoint and about thirty men, some police, some just armed civilians. When the commandos saw so many vehicles together, they must have realized we'd spotted them and they ran off quickly and hid somewhere over there.' He pointed to some undulating folds in the landscape not more than three hundred metres away and I wandered over there with him. To the west the land fell sharply into the dry bed of a wadi that evidently ran into the Euphrates – hence the bridge, which formed a culvert across the road. On the opposite side of the road, the north side, I could see the lush greenness of the river valley, the spiky heads of palm trees and tamarisks, and beyond them clear across to the other bank. To my immediate south-west was a line of traditional-looking rural houses, which might have been the habitation McNab mentions. Further west, past the houses, a graded track of some kind appeared to run parallel to the wadi we stood near.

Ahmad pointed west, past the houses. 'That was where we stopped,' he said. 'On that track about five hundred metres from here. Rather than attack them, we thought the best bet was to surround them and cut off their escape, so we jumped out of the vehicles over there and spread out along the track. As we did that, they started shooting.'

Remembering that McNab said the Iraqis had initiated the firefight as soon as the vehicles came to a halt – and bearing in mind that the SAS were short of ammunition – I quizzed him again over this. 'No, I'm certain it was them who opened fire,' he said. 'Our object was to capture them, not to kill them.'

'Were any of your men hit?'

'No. No one was hit. They only fired a few shots and we fired back in a salvo. It went on for about ten minutes. They went silent and we thought we might have hit them, but we weren't sure so we didn't come straight across the wadi – we worked our way round the houses in a big circle. When we got here, though, there was no one. They had got away.'

I looked at the road to my right, recalling that McNab said they had crossed a road. Surely, I thought, with the bright moonlight and the place full of traffic, that would have been a big risk. Ahmad was reading my thoughts. 'I don't think they went across the road,' he said. 'I think they went through the culvert. They must have known that it led down to the Euphrates, and anyway, that's where we caught them eventually. But at the time we knew we'd lost them and we didn't follow. It was only later that we heard they'd been spotted by other people down by the river. And we threw a cordon round it.'

I wondered about McNab's statement that he had seen the lights of Abu Kamal in Syria and since this was, according to Ahmad, the furthest Bravo Two Zero had got west on this side of the road, I asked him if it was possible to see Syria from any place near here.

He shook his head. 'It's too far away,' he said. 'More than ten kilometres. You can't see Abu Kamal from here.'

I also quizzed Ahmad about S60s – had any gunners opened fire on the patrol?

'There were air-raids on that night,' he said. 'And the anti-air-craft batteries did fire at some aircraft going over, but not at the British commandos. That would have been stupid, anyway, because S60s fire explosive shells and it would have endangered the local people –

there are plenty of houses here. No, they only fired at the enemy air-craft, I'm sure of that.'

In this instance, Ryan backs up McNab's story that S60s opened up on them, no doubt repeating what McNab had said at the debriefing after the war, and says that in fact it was quite helpful for the patrol because it made the Iraqis believe an air-raid was on and obliged them to keep their heads down. Could it be that McNab believed the AA guns were firing at his patrol, when in fact they had opened up on enemy aircraft instead?

Ryan does, however, describe the second attempt at a hijacking which Ahmad had told me about, but which McNab does not mention. He says that the patrol made three successive attempts to stop cars, but that the drivers were roaring past 'like madmen'.

# CHAPTER
# thirteen

AFTER THE POLICE HAD LOST THE SAS men by the road,
Ahmad said, reports had come through that they had been spotted
down by the Euphrates, and local citizens had been alerted and organized into groups to cordon off the area and prevent their escape. These
were not part of any formal militia, he explained, just solid local people
who felt it was their duty to help the police. Later that night Ahmad
had been with a group of policemen who had shot and captured one
of the British commandos. Since, as far as I knew, Mike Coburn was
the only member of the patrol injured in the contacts that night, I
assumed he was the one Ahmad was referring to.

FOR WHAT HAPPENED TO THE SAS patrol after they had
eluded the police that night, we have to rely on McNab's account.

When they came under fire by the S60 battery, he says, the patrol crossed a road into a built-up area that led down to the banks of the Euphrates. Passing through the estate as silently as ghosts, they came across cultivation trails that led down to the river about 150 metres away. They holed up in a plantation, and McNab sent two men to fill all the water-bottles in the river, ready for a final push. When they returned, the five of them considered their options. They could withdraw to the east, lie up for the following day and have another crack at the border tomorrow night, or they could head north, crossing the river. They could press on west and make a final play for the border the same night as a patrol, or they could split up and every man take his chance. Pulling back to the east was out, they decided, because the area was too densely populated to hide in for another day. As for the river, it was in spate after the snow and rain, and its edges rimmed with ice: in their debilitated condition they would have lasted about ten minutes in the freezing waters, McNab reckoned.

The only other option was to make a last-ditch attempt to reach Syria together that night. They started off, patrolling tactically in file, moving parallel with the Euphrates, seeing headlights streaming over a bridge in the distance. Soon they came across a deep wadi which seemed to curve round to the west, their direction of march. A good 25 metres deep, the wadi would protect them from view and, with any luck, would take them as far as the border. McNab left the others spaced out, lying as still as statues, and crawled over the lip of the wadi to recce it. On the opposite side he saw the silhouette of a sentry stamping his feet and, behind him, to his astonishment, what appeared to be an enemy command centre: tents, buildings, vehicles, radio antennae, and many soldiers. He made his way back

to where Coburn was lying and the two turned to crawl back to the patrol, coming into a semi-crouch position as they made the nearest ditch. At that moment the sentries across the wadi spotted them, and all hell let loose.

Coburn hit the deck and fired off bursts from his Minimi at any muzzle-flashes he could see. McNab blasted away with his last 203 grenades and ran, heading desperately back to the banks of the Euphrates, hearing the other three letting rip with their own Minimis and 203s, but not sure where they were. He and Coburn lay in the bushes on the riverbank about ten metres below the ploughed fields. Their backs were to the river, but there was no way they were going to attempt to cross it, McNab said. When four Iraqis came cautiously along the bank towards them, he and Coburn bumped them and legged it west across a ploughed field. From the road to the south there came the sound of yelling and blazing lights. McNab popped his head inquisitively through a hedgerow, only to find himself challenged by an Iraqi, whom Coburn shot to pieces with his Minimi. McNab blatted away with his rifle, covering Coburn as he scrambled through the hedge. They retreated fast, but the area was now buzzing with activity.

It was about 0400 hours and only two hours of darkness remained. If they did not penetrate the Syrian frontier before first light, McNab knew, they were as good as finished. They shimmied over a six-foot-high chain-link fence and found themselves facing a massive convoy of vehicles: trucks, Land-Cruisers and armoured personnel carriers, parked along a road. Half the Iraqi army, it must have felt like, had been assigned to kill or capture Bravo Two Zero that night. McNab spotted a five-metre gap between two trucks and they decided to make a dash through it. As they cleared another

fence a soldier stuck his head out of a truck window. McNab shot him, then fired a burst into the back of the truck and lobbed an L2 grenade for good measure: 'the sounds of screaming filled the night' was the result. On the opposite side of the road they blasted away until they ran out of ammunition – which lasted 'all of five seconds', McNab says – then dropped their useless weapons and ran off across some garbage pits where small fires smouldered. As they did so, two AK 47s opened up on them. Coburn was hit and went down, while McNab raced off to the right, believing that the Kiwi was dead. He was still confident, telling himself that he was now through the last contact and that there were only four kilometres to go. In normal circumstances he could have run that in twenty minutes.

WE DROVE BACK THROUGH Krabilah, taking a right turn down to the river through a patchwork of cultivated fields where pumps rattled and thumped turning iron wheels on antique fan-belts to irrigate the reddish earth. Ahmad told Abbas to stop by a muddy field lying on the banks of a wadi which curved east down towards the river. The wadi was a deep one; beyond it I could see the green heads of palms and eucalyptus lining the Euphrates.

Ahmad showed me a ditch running along the verge between the road and the field, about a metre deep. 'This is where we were,' he said. 'There were seven or eight of us, all police. We had a couple of Land-Cruisers with us which were parked on the road. We had been alerted that the British commandos had been spotted in this area, and we were ready for them, here in the ditch. Suddenly a man came crawling over the lip of the wadi towards us and we shouted at him to stop. He didn't so we opened fire. He was carrying only a bayonet, which he dropped

when we started shooting. He screamed out some thing in English. I told the men to stop firing and I went over to him, followed by a few others. He was badly wounded in the foot and the arm, and blood was pouring out – he had sort of turned over on his side by the time we got there. We searched him to make sure he had no more weapons, then we lifted him up to take him to the vehicle. He was shivering from the cold and shock, and when he was in the Land-Cruiser I wrapped him in a blanket. He said, "Thank you," in English.

'We took him straight to the hospital, where the doctor examined him and said he had lost a lot of blood and needed a transfusion. He asked for volunteers. I offered to give blood but I was the wrong blood group. Two of my companions also offered blood and one was accepted. He was given a transfusion and the doctor said it saved his life.'

This was interesting because McNab says that Coburn was treated very differently on his way to captivity, stating that the policemen in the vehicles roared with laughter every time the vehicle went over a bump, sending crippling pain through his wounded ankle. In fact, McNab does not even mention that Coburn was taken to a hospital at all, and denies that he received medical treatment at all for his foot, which he says was just left to heal by itself. He says that the Kiwi was chained naked to a bed and left to rot, and that his captors would regularly torture him by putting pressure on his wounds.

I asked Ahmad if the prisoner had been mistreated on the way to the hospital. He shook his head. 'We had very strict orders not to molest prisoners,' he said. 'Not just these men, I mean, but any prisoners. Anyone – certainly anyone who was not an officer – would have got into big trouble if he had touched them without permission. And this man was seriously wounded – he would have died

without a transfusion. Of course, I can't say what happened when he left the hospital, but I know he got the best treatment there.'

I recalled the story of an SAS warrant officer who had been captured by the Iraqis in a separate operation in the Gulf War. His leg had been badly smashed up by gunshot wounds, but he had been operated on by a British-trained Iraqi surgeon, who had done such a brilliant job on his leg that when he was repatriated he had needed no further treatment. Ahmad's story of offering blood, and the doctor's anxiousness to save Coburn's life seemed to be consistent with that, and all the little details – the blanket, the way he was lifted by the police – seemed to ring true.

That he was taken to a hospital and given a transfusion was confirmed that night by a man named Zayid, who had been a medical orderly at the hospital on 26 January 1991, and who was introduced to me by Al-Haj Nur ad-Din, the teashop-owner who had found me Ahmad. 'It's true he was given a transfusion,' Zayid said. 'And he wasn't mistreated, although I did accuse him of being an Israeli, and he got very angry about that, saying, "No! No! English! English!" But no one beat him up or anything. Why would they?'

'You might have been angry about the people he and his comrades had killed and injured – your own people.'

Zayid looked at me in surprise. 'But no one was killed,' he said, 'and if anyone had been injured they would have been brought to the hospital and I would have known. The only one brought to the hospital was this man.'

I asked Ahmad if he could verify this. 'There was no one killed that night,' he confirmed. 'There wasn't anyone injured – nothing. I was at the hospital too, so I also would have known if anyone else had been hurt. The Englishman was the only one injured – one of the

commandos was killed, of course, but there were none of our men in the hospital. This is a small place and I knew all the policemen who were on duty that night. I can tell you that not one Iraqi was killed or injured by the commandos, and you can ask anyone you like.'

I actually went about in my spare moments over the next two days doing just that. Though almost everyone who had been here ten years previously appeared to know about Bravo Two Zero and the gun-battle, no one recalled any Iraqis having been shot.


THAT NIGHT I THOUGHT OVER WHAT Ahmad and the others had told me. I was reluctant to believe that McNab and his men hadn't caused any casualties at all, but again, what would be the profit in the Iraqis lying about it? After all, if your house gets broken into by a burglar who takes your priceless stamp collection, there is little to be gained by claiming that nothing is missing. If this was a propaganda ploy, then surely it had misfired – it would clearly have been to the Iraqis' advantage to maintain that Bravo Two Zero had killed even more than they had, in order to justify some of Saddam Hussein's excesses during the war, and certainly they had taken every opportunity to gain the world's sympathy by publicizing the deaths of Iraqi civilians and children in the Amiriya Bunker in Baghdad.

McNab says in his book that intelligence sources revealed later that his eight-man patrol had accounted for at least 250 Iraqi casualties during their operation, which, for McNab's group, lasted from 22 January to 27 January. In effect, though, the active period ran only between 1600 hours on 24 January and the early hours of 27 January – less than three days. Apart from the alleged shoot-out at the VCP, the only major contacts McNab relates are the firefight near

Abbas's farm and the series of gun-battles here in Krabilah between sunset on 26 January and sunrise the following morning.

I tried to apply some simple addition to the process. At the 'Abbas shoot-out' McNab claimed fifteen killed and many more wounded, so for the sake of argument I assumed that the total count was about 45. There were also the three guards at the checkpoint to take into consideration – a theoretical total of 48. Even if these contacts happened just as McNab describes them, and bearing in mind that all the evidence from eyewitnesses suggested that there were no Iraqi casualties during either incident, the number of deaths still only amounted to about a fifth of the total McNab stated. That meant that in the final encounter at Krabilah – less, of course, anyone Ryan and his group accounted for independently – the SAS must have taken out up to two hundred men. Ryan stated that Consiglio himself came up against twelve men in his contact, so assuming that he hit them all – though there is no evidence that he hit *any* – that still left about 188 bodies unaccounted for.

What troubled me most, though, was the question of ammunition. McNab constantly emphasized how little the patrol had. Half of the original amount had been used up in the initial firefight, and after the second contact on 26 January, he himself had about one and a half magazines left and Coburn a hundred rounds of link for the Minimi, a total of about a hundred and forty-five rounds between them. Legs and Dinger had thirty rounds of link for the machine-gun and one magazine – sixty rounds in all. No one knows how many rounds Bob Consiglio had, but let us average it out at fifty: that makes a sum total of about 250 rounds for the whole patrol. Although the SAS may be good shots, even the best marksman in the world cannot hit a target every round in a combat situation. A hit every ten shots is

a pretty good average, but the idea that the patrol, weak, exhausted, under extreme pressure and fighting at night, could have hit an Iraqi every 1.25 shots beggars belief. Peter Ratcliffe, for one, has challenged the claim. This veteran of 25 years' experience with the Regiment has pointed out that, according to current military theory, it would take a battalion of five hundred to destroy an enemy company of one hundred, and at least 1250 men to take out 250. 'Actually,' Ratcliffe added wryly, 'it is a great pity that McNab was captured and Ryan escaped, because otherwise – at the rate they were killing Iraqis – the war might have been over in a week.'

# CHAPTER
## fourteen

THE CONTACT WITH THE SENTRIES at McNab's 'command centre' was the point at which the patrol finally fragmented into three: McNab and Coburn, Dinger and Lane, and Consiglio. I had accounted for the capture of one of them – Coburn – and now I began to look for eyewitnesses who could tell me about the others. Al-Haj Nur ad-Din, the engineer turned teashop-owner, told me that he knew of at least two men who had been involved in the capture of one of the British commandos on Rummani, an island in the Euphrates facing Krabilah. This immediately rang true, because I knew that Lane and Dinger had swum across the Euphrates to an island, unnamed in either Ryan's or McNab's texts, where they had taken refuge in a pump-house. Nur ad-Din said that he knew the actual pump-house involved and offered to take me across to Rummani and show it to me.

SINCE DINGER HAS PRODUCED NO public record of the events of that night, we have to rely once again on Ryan and McNab. After the contact at the deep wadi, McNab says, Dinger and Legs, now separated from the others, realized that they could never fight their way through with their limited ammunition. Although they had previously rejected the idea of crossing the river, it was now their only option. At the water's edge they tried, with no success, to unchain a small boat, so instead they launched themselves into the icy waters of the Euphrates. The water was so cold it took their breath away, but they swam about a hundred metres across to a sand spit, where they lay quaking and gasping for a long time.

The only way off the spit was past a pontoon bridge, about 250 metres to their west, on which they could see a roadblock. From the south bank there came sporadic firing and the play of flashlights on the water. Their camouflage suits were already freezing on them, and if they remained where they were, they would soon be dead. There was no choice but to try and breast the main river, which was about five hundred metres across. They found a polystyrene box, which they broke up and stuffed into their smocks, then they waded out into the water and started to swim. The cold sapped their energy, and they let their weapons slip out of their hands. By the time they touched bottom on the other side, they had been carried a kilometre and a half downstream, and Legs was incapable of wading ashore. Dinger found a small pump-house on the bank and dragged his friend into it. He began to heat some water with his last Hexamine block, but it was too late – Legs was no longer *compos mentis* and he knocked the mug of steaming liquid aside.

At first light, Dinger pulled his comrade into the sunlight. The fields by the river were already full of Fellahin, the sedentary peasants

of the Euphrates and Tigris valleys, and according to both Ryan and McNab, Dinger deliberately surrendered to one of them, who locked them in the hut. When the man ran off to tell others, Dinger broke out and made off, only to run into a big gang of local people, who surrounded him, knocked him down and tied him up. One of the men pulled a knife and threatened to cut off his ear, but at this point Dinger brought out his gold sovereigns, which the crowd fought over. He was rescued from them by a group of soldiers, who had evidently, McNab said, had orders to capture him alive.

He was taken across the river in a convoy and delivered to a camp, where he was severely beaten. While he was there, Legs was brought in on a stretcher and put into an ambulance. He was completely motionless, and Dinger feared that his comrade was dead. That was the last he ever saw of him.

This must be the account Dinger gave at the debrief afterwards, for Ryan's version is virtually identical, except for a few details – significantly, in view of what Ahmad had told me, that it was the police rather than the army who took him away, and a police station rather than a camp in which he last saw Legs.


NUR AD-DIN GUIDED ME THROUGH the streets of Krabilah, turning off on a road which led down to the pontoon bridge which is mentioned at least twice in McNab's account. Slightly east of the bridge was a landing-place where several ancient and battered-looking boats were moored, and I wondered if it was one of these same vessels that Dinger and Legs had tried to cut loose that night. Standing at the water's edge, I saw that the bridge was about 250 metres west of the landing-place. At first I concluded that this must have

been where they set off from, but when Nur ad-Din reminded me that the river had been much higher in January 1991, I guessed that the landing-place itself must have been the spit of land on which they had lain freezing in the darkness. Ahmad told me that a weapon, still loaded, had been recovered from the river the day after the incident, a little downstream from here, confirming that the SAS men had indeed let go of their firearms. I was later able to see that weapon – a Minimi light machine-gun – in Baghdad.

After a great deal of bargaining, we managed to hire a steel canoe from one of the friendly but dishevelled boatmen at the landing-place, and pushed off downstream towards Rummani. The Euphrates bore little resemblance to the fearsome torrent it must have been in January 1991. It was deep blue and utterly tranquil, bordered by lush thickets of phragmites reeds and tussocks of halfa grass, where egrets and herons roosted and pied kingfishers hovered. The current was strong and I could feel the water pulling at the vessel as the boatman fought to swing it round towards the shore of Rummani.

Suddenly Nur ad-Din pointed to a squat cabin of grey breeze-blocks standing a good fifty metres from the shore-line on a rise among clumps of high bushes. 'That's it!' he told me. 'That's the place.'

The boatman looped around, surfing the current, and brought us in to the swampy shore. In January 1991, of course, the water-line would have been much higher and nearer to the cabin. It was only a few minutes' walk to the hut, a crudely built structure with a gaping hole in the wall through which I could see a greasy pump-engine – now silent – attached to a pipe that obviously fed water into a catch-basin outside, from where it was chanelled

to fields of wheat and apricot orchards beyond. There was a thin steel door at the back and I entered, crouching on the oil-saturated floor to spend a few minutes in silent meditation for Steven Lane, a courageous British soldier who had spent his last hours here. I knew I must be the first of Lane's own tribe to visit the place since his death.

There was no one about, but Nur ad-Din led me across a field of golden wheat to an orchard, where children began to gather excitedly round us, showing us a gigantic – and poisonous – green snake they had just killed. We asked if there were any adults around and eventually a thickset old man appeared, a tremendously powerful-looking individual in a ragged dishdasha and knotted shamagh. I told him that I was interested in the British soldiers who had hidden in the pump-house ten years ago and he nodded vigorously. 'I remember that morning,' he said. 'I was with some others and we saw a foreigner lurking in the bushes. Someone fired a shot over his head and he gave himself up. He was unarmed except for a knife – I think he had some grenades with him – and we tied his arms behind his back and took him off to the police headquarters in Krabilah on a tractor.'

'Was he beaten up?' I asked.

'No, not at all. We pushed him down on his knees, tied him and searched him for weapons – he was carrying a bayonet and two grenades. But nobody touched him apart from that.'

'Did anyone threaten to cut off his ear?'

'No, of course not.'

'Did he give you any gold?'

'I know nothing about gold.'

'What about the other man – the one in the pump-house?'

'He was dying of cold when they found him. He was still alive when they took him away, though.'

I cross-questioned the old man, whose name was Mohammed, carefully over the next hour, but he stuck resolutely to his story, that Dinger had not been beaten by his captors. In the end I was satisfied he was telling the truth about this, although I wasn't certain about the gold sovereigns – he shifted niftily away from the subject whenever I came back to it. Finally, I asked him if he would swear by God that Dinger was not beaten. The great British Arabist Gertrude Bell wrote that the Fellahin of Iraq traditionally placed great store in oaths by God, which were considered blasphemy if the swearer were not telling the truth. 'All who hear the oath,' she wrote, 'know beyond question that if the speaker is foresworn, his temerity will bring upon him within the year a judgement greater and more inexorable than that of man.'

Mohammed swore quite readily in front of the large crowd that had collected around us. When I had finished the interview, he brought me a huge dish of fresh apricots.

I stayed on Rummani until the evening, reluctant to return to the noise and dust of Krabilah. It felt like a world left behind by the modern age, a small enclave of tradition, a haven of peace. For the Fellahin who lived here – the settled, farming tribes of the Euphrates – life cannot have changed much since Babylonian times. They live in the same mud-built houses, use the same tools and live by much the same laws as they did in the days of Hammurabi. The influence of the rivers – the Tigris and the Euphrates – is dominant in the lives of these peasants, and throughout the millennia they have been exposed to the incursions of invaders from the deserts. Their history is one of unending struggle against nature and against outsiders –

to them, with six thousand years' uninterrupted existence along this shore, the SAS must have been no more than just another bunch of 'barbarian invaders'.

I sat by the pump-house until the sun turned the sky transparent gold and the blue waters of the river became oil-black, watching fishing smacks drifting lazily on the current and kingfishers hovering and diving. By evening, a considerable number of Fellahin had collected, anxious to find out what was happening, and many of them appeared to know the story of Legs and Dinger. It had become a local legend – even children who weren't born then had heard the tale. I found one young man, Farraj, a solid-looking, articulate youth of about twenty, who told me he had been with the men who had captured Dinger, and had seen Legs in the pump-house. 'I was only a boy then,' he said. 'But I remember it like yesterday. It was mid-morning, I think, when they spotted this man in the fields wearing camouflage, and someone fired over his head with an AK47. He stopped at once and put his hands up and we surrounded him and tied his hands behind his back. He didn't try to fight, and he wasn't carrying any weapons, except maybe a knife – or a bayonet – and some grenades. There were no policemen involved. We put him on a tractor and took him across the river to the police station – it had to be a tractor because it was the only vehicle that could cross the ford.'

'Were the men here already looking for him? Did they know the hunt was on for these commandos?'

'No, we only knew about it afterwards.'

'Then how come someone was walking around with an AK47?'

'Everyone here has weapons – it's illegal, but nobody bothers. When they spotted the man someone just went into his house and got his rifle.'

'But didn't you hear a lot of firing the previous night?'

'No, nothing.'

'Was the man beaten up when he was captured?'

'Not at all. They forced him down on his knees and tied his hands, but nothing more.'

'What about the other commando – the one in the pump-house?'

'I was with the group who went to get him and I saw him lying in the hut. He was in a bad way, you could tell, and his eyes were totally lifeless. The men I was with carried him out of the hut and lit a fire, hoping that it would save him, but he cringed away from the flames, probably thinking they meant to burn him. He was put on a stretcher and taken across the river, but I am sure he was still alive at that time.'

# CHAPTER
## fifteen

LIKE THE ARMY OF ANCIENT SPARTA, an SAS patrol is built on a complement of pairs – the buddy-buddy system – which is one of the reasons David Stirling reduced the basic patrol unit from his original concept of five to four. Bravo Two Zero was essentially two four-man patrols welded together for a single job. When the patrol ran into a wall of fire at the wadi on the night of 26 January, the instinct was to fragment into pairs, leaving Bob Consiglio, who was last man, or tail-end Charlie, on his own. Later, Legs and Dinger heard several contacts going on – one of them an extended firefight with a Minimi, followed by silence, which they assumed was Bob's last stand. McNab says that Bob went forward and tried to fight his way out of a contact, but was hit in the head by a round that came out of his stomach and ignited a phosphorus grenade in his webbing, dying instantly. Ryan reports that Bob held off the Iraqis for

thirty minutes single-handedly, and assumes that he took out many Iraqis before he finally ran out of ammunition and was killed.

AHMAD TOLD ME THAT ON THE morning of 27 January, he had seen the body of one of the British commandos, badly burned, lying in the middle of a track that led down to the Euphrates. He said that there was a local citizen, a lawyer named Subhi, who had been present at the time the SAS man had been shot. In fact, Subhi was one of those who had shot him. Subhi turned out to be the very opposite of the gracious Ahmad. Small, powerful and tight-lipped, he spoke in a sibilant whisper and looked like everyone's idea of a villain out of *The Arabian Nights*. Nevertheless, he was frank and articulate and I had no reason to believe he was telling me anything but the truth.

He and Ahmad took me to the place where Bob had been shot. The track meandered through some ancient ruins – a shapeless and unidentifiable mound of baked mud – and turned sharply at right angles past a narrow feeder canal down to a few mud-brick houses and a grove of trees at the water's edge. The Euphrates was near – perhaps two hundred metres away – but that winter it must have been much higher. Ahmad demonstrated how the commando had been lying, face-up, in the middle of the track. This surprised me, because I had imagined Bob dying surrounded by the corpses of the enemies he had felled. While Ryan definitely gives this impression, McNab merely says that Bob fought his way aggressively out of a contact, and that seemed to be nearer to the facts – at least as indicated by the site of his body.

'It was about two o'clock on the morning of 27 January,' Subhi

told me, 'when we saw this man running towards us down the track. I was one of seven local citizens, most of us armed, who had been collected to help the police encircle this area. The foreign soldiers had been seen down here and the police were trying to cut them off. We were in that copse of trees over there by the building, quite near the water's edge, and we saw this figure running towards us down the track. We shouted out to him to stop, and he shouted back something in a weak voice. Then he turned as if to go back and we opened fire. Some bullets hit him and he fell down on the track. We opened fire again. One of the rounds must have hit a grenade he had in his equipment, because it exploded and continued to burn, and all the time he was screaming words in English. He might have been trying to surrender, but none of us knew English and we weren't sure. To tell you the truth, we were a bit nervous. The rambling went on for about a quarter of an hour and then it stopped. We didn't go near him, though, until it was light. Then the police came and took the body away. It was badly burned, especially around the chest, and his equipment was burned too. He had taken a bullet in the mouth, which had probably spun him round, and another bullet had probably ignited the grenade in his pouch.'

'How did you feel about shooting him?'

'I was doing what I was asked to do by the government, and no one told those soldiers to enter our country. On the other hand, I was sorry, because I felt he might have been trying to surrender and we were really too nervous to take chances.'

I had to bite my lip at this. Bob had died a brave man's death – a hero's death – but had it really been necessary? After all, four of the patrol were captured by the Iraqis, and though they went through interrogation and torture, all of them had lived to tell the tale, to see

their families, and even to soldier on in the Regiment. Once McNab's group had hijacked the taxi, they had been drawn into an impenetrable net of roads and checkpoints and habitations from which it was virtually impossible to escape as a group. McNab's best move, probably, would have been to surrender at the VCP. Of course it is easy to be wise with hindsight, but the tremendous imperative not to get captured was, as it turned out, misplaced. It was partly pure chauvinism, partly fear engendered by Allied propaganda about Iraqi interrogation methods and the use of 'human shields', which proved to be exaggerated. McNab says that the SAS dreaded the idea of being captured by the Iraqis and says he had read reports of atrocities they had carried out against POWs in the Iran-Iraq war, including flogging, electrocution and partial dismemberment.

Though no one can dispute the courage of those who endured the Iraqi jails, at least all the prisoners survived.

# CHAPTER
# sixteen

FAYADH ABDALLAH WAS AN illiterate Fellah of about sixty who
lived at a former British oil-station called 'T1', outside Krabilah. His
name had been given to me by the police sergeant major, Ahmad, as
the man who had discovered one of the British commandos on the
morning of 27 January 1991 in an irrigation pipe by the Euphrates,
not far from the Syrian border. I met Fayadh at the restaurant opposite
my hotel in Krabilah for a preliminary chat and found him a simple
man, obviously overawed by the occasion. His face had been whittled
away by years in the sun and wind, his body honed down by hard work,
so that only the bare minimum remained. Fayadh confirmed that he
had indeed discovered a foreigner in combat dress hidden down by the
river on that day, and since I had already accounted for the deaths or
capture of Lane, Consiglio, Dinger and Coburn, I knew that the soldier in question could only be McNab.

WHILE LEGS AND DINGER WERE making their way painfully to Rummani, McNab writes, he was pressing on towards the border across ice-crusted fields. He was only about four kilometres away from Syria and freedom, but dawn was coming and he knew he would never make it in daylight. Instead, he crawled into an irrigation culvert under a steel plate and lay there in the water, prepared to wait out the day. Early that morning, as he lay shivering in the pipe, he writes, an old goatherder approached and hung around the culvert for a few moments, allowing McNab to get a glimpse of him. The goatherd disappeared and McNab thought he hadn't been compromised, but a little later some motor vehicles screeched to a halt nearby. Suddenly men began to scream and shoot off their weapons madly into the steel plate above him and McNab knew the game was up.

He was pulled out of the culvert by 'gibbering, jabbering' soldiers who were, according to him, in an unbelievable frenzy. They made him kneel and suddenly laid into him brutally, kicking and thumping his body, pulling his hair, screaming at him. They gave him 'thudding instep kicks' to his head, and 'telling well-aimed toe-cap blows' to his kidneys, mouth and ears, until he was coughing up blood. He was thrown into a Land-Cruiser, hit on the head with a rifle butt and exposed to wildly excited crowds who yelled obscenities at him, spat on him, slapped and punched him savagely. This was probably, McNab says, because they held him personally responsible for their dead and wounded friends and family members. 'There was a gagging stench of unwashed bodies,' he writes. 'It was like a horror film with zombies.' [24]

Eventually he was taken to a compound and dragged inside the gate, where he saw Dinger, whose head was swollen to the size of a football and whose equipment was covered in blood.

FAYADH TOOK ME TO AN AREA of fields and irrigated plots on the western side of the Rummani pontoon bridge, not far from the Syrian border. Here, he showed me an irrigation pipe joining two fields, over which ran a mud track. There were modern concrete structures about five hundred metres away to the south, and beyond them, the asphalt road. I examined the pipe, which was half buried and obviously not wide enough to take a human body. 'This is not the same pipe that was here then,' Fayadh said. 'There was a bigger pipe in the same place, but this area is part of the flood plain in the summer and the pipes get damaged or go rusty. The original pipe has been replaced.'

'So this was where you found the British soldier?'

'Yes. It was about noon. I was going about my work as usual, clearing out the irrigation ditches. I passed by this pipe and I noticed that there was a man inside it. I was really surprised, because I had never seen anything like that before. I didn't know who it was, whether a bandit or what.'

'You didn't know there had been shooting here the night before, and that the police were looking for enemy soldiers?'

'No, I had no idea about that. I didn't know who the stranger was, but I knew something odd was going on and I didn't want the responsibility of dealing with it myself. There was a temporary police post in some tents up there . . .' He pointed south, to a place about five hundred metres away. 'And I ran off there as fast as I could. The police came back in their vehicles and pulled the man out. It was a foreigner, not a big man or heavily built, but quite fit-looking, who didn't seem to be suffering much from the cold.'

'Did the police fire into the pipe from above?'

'No. They fired off a few shots in the air in excitement, because

162

they had obviously been looking for him, but they didn't shoot into the ground or into the pipe.'

'Did they beat him up – kick him in the head, for instance?'

'No. They didn't kick him or beat him at any time while I was present. They made him kneel down, tied his hands and searched him. I think he did have a knife – a bayonet – and they also found some stuff they said was explosives wrapped in brown paper. After that somebody brought him water in a bowl, but he refused to drink, and then someone else gave him a cup of tea from a vacuum flask, holding it to his lips. He must have thought it was poison or some-thing, because he kept turning his head away. Someone else sipped it to show him it was all right. He seemed quite nervous. After that the police took him off in their vehicle, but I never saw anyone beat him or hit him at all.'

'Are you absolutely certain of that?'

'Yes.'

'Would you swear it by God?'

'Yes, I do swear it by God. No one mistreated that man. The police fired in the air, yes, and later when they took him to the car some women ululated – that is our custom – but no one hit him or beat him up. On the contrary, they treated him well and gave him water as I said.'

I really had no way of knowing if what Fayadh had told me was true, but I simply could not believe that this emaciated old man could be part of a government conspiracy. He evidently hadn't even realized there was a war going on at the time.

The idea that the Iraqis had brought McNab tea rather than kick-ing him half to death seemed much more in keeping with what I had seen of their character – indeed, with the Arab character in general as

I had experienced it for two decades. My mentor, the great British Arabist and explorer Sir Wilfred Thesiger, who served with David Stirling in the original SAS during World War II, wrote that the Bedouin in particular had such great respect for human dignity that they would rather kill a man than humiliate him. No one can doubt that Saddam Hussein and his cronies in government have been responsible for heinous acts. Even against his own people, Saddam has perpetrated forced relocation and deportation, summary arrest, deprivation, torture, detention, political execution and genocide. But the men and women McNab describes were ordinary Iraqis, lineal heirs of a great civilization, who had no need to go on a feeding frenzy over a few foreign troops in their territory when they had been fighting off invaders since the time of Cain and Abel.

If what I had been told was true, Coburn, Lane and McNab had all been shown some small acts of humanity during their capture by the very people McNab says acted like primitive savages. As for the implication that they held him and his patrol responsible for the large number of locals he says they killed or injured, I could find no evidence of a single kill, or even an injury inflicted on the citizens of Krabilah by Bravo Two Zero on 26 to 27 January 1991.

# CHAPTER
# seventeen

THE MARKAZ KRABILAH, OR POLICE headquarters, to which
Adnan Badawi had reported the five British commandos on the evening
of 26 January lay not much more than a kilometre away from the place
where McNab had been captured. Judging by the short distance he
appears to have been taken by vehicle, this is probably where he was
held and interrogated for the first 'tactical phase' of his captivity.
Though McNab himself describes the place as a 'commando camp',
Ahmad told me that there were no Iraqi commandos in Krabilah at
the time, and that the capture of the enemy troops was purely a police
matter. Ryan also says that Dinger was taken to a police station, and
since Dinger was almost the first person McNab saw on arrival, it is
clear that it was the same place. In any case, the sketch and description of McNab's commando camp in his book are uncannily like the
police headquarters in Krabilah.

Unfortunately, though, this was where the trail went cold for me. I was sure that somebody in Krabilah must have been present when McNab, Dinger and Coburn were interrogated, but I was denied access to either people or places. Uday, at the Ministry of Information, had told me that this was because the administration had been changed completely since 1991 and the records lost. Although I knew this was true to some extent – no less than eighteen tons of Iraqi records had been captured by the Kurds in 1992-3, for example – I didn't swallow it. I suspected, rightly or wrongly, that it was because the Iraqis were aware that in their interrogation and treatment of the SAS patrol they had breached the Geneva Convention, and did not welcome my prying Mk I eyeball ten years later.

Although McNab says otherwise in his book, Iraq is a signatory of the Fourth Geneva Convention (1949), which requires humane treatment of prisoners of war and protection from violence, intimidation, insults and public curiosity. Article 17 of the Convention explicitly prohibits the infliction of physical or mental torture or any other form of coercion on prisoners to secure information, and prisoners who refuse to provide information may not be threatened, insulted or exposed to unpleasant treatment of any kind. Clearly, however, Iraq did violate the Convention during the war, not only in its treatment of POWs, but also in its murder, rape and torture of Kuwaiti citizens. The Convention is, of course, only a piece of paper – it was regularly violated by the Americans in Vietnam and has been flouted by the Israelis for the past two decades.

The SAS are 'prone-to-capture' troops, and every SAS man knows that in the real world he can expect to be tortured if captured, and not only by the Iraqis. It is for this reason that a 'resistance to

interrogation' component forms part of the Regiment's selection process. In practice, all armies use 'tactical questioning', which involves some type of coercion or 'unpleasant treatment' – among the least pleasant and most effective being sensory deprivation and deprivation of sleep, rather than pulling out fingernails.

I have no doubt that McNab and the other three members of his patrol who were captured were beaten, deprived, manhandled, insulted, humiliated, abused and disoriented during their weeks in Iraqi jails. I also think it is possible that some of their captors persecuted them for no other reason than pure pleasure. One cannot help feeling that McNab was justified in his threat to 'slot' those Iraqis who mistreated him if he ever ran into them again.

No brutal treatment of POWs is acceptable, either morally or under the Geneva Convention, but the question of the extent of McNab's mistreatment by the Iraqis has already been raised by a fellow detainee, Stan. Speaking during the Auckland trial over Coburn's book *Soldier Five*, Stan swore under oath that some of the more extreme scenes McNab describes in *Bravo Two Zero* were fantasy. Having turned up in the Baghdad holding centre only a few days after McNab, Stan must have found out what had happened to him at the time, or discovered it later during the debrief. He specifies in particular that McNab's story that he was burned with a red-hot spoon and had his teeth pulled out during interrogation was incorrect. In McNab's account, the Iraqi dentist – a veteran of nine years at Guy's Hospital, London – violates his Hippocratic oath by wrenching his teeth out without anaesthetic, to the cackling of an interrogator who demands, 'Did you really think we're going to help you, you despicable heap of shit?' [25] Yet why should it have been so unlikely that the Iraqis would help him? As McNab

167

himself has one of his captors admit, Coburn received two pints of blood from the Iraqis in the process of having his elbow operated on, and the SAS warrant officer captured with a broken leg had it expertly fixed.

One remarkable aspect of McNab's incarceration – and one that must inwardly have convinced him that the Iraqis did not really mean business – was that he was allowed to associate with his colleagues, first Dinger, then, after he had been moved to Baghdad, with Coburn and Stan. As McNab must have known well, this is a big no-no for interrogators, since there is nothing guaranteed to break an individual more quickly than the feeling that he is totally isolated. Allowing the SAS men to congregate was certain to raise their morale, and also gave them the opportunity to compare notes and perfect their cover story.

One cannot fail to applaud the courage and grit shown by the SAS men who were detained by the Iraqis, but it is worth observing again that all of them survived the experience at least well enough to continue serving with the Regiment. In his autobiography *Immediate Action*, McNab describes how, during the escape and evasion phase of his selection for 22 SAS, he and his comrades were briefed by a former female SOE agent who had been captured by the Germans in World War II, had been kept in solitary confinement for weeks in freezing conditions, and was continuously burned, raped and abused by the Gestapo. Another survivor, a former British infantry corporal, had been captured in the Korean war and force-marched across north Korea, was beaten continuously until he lost all his teeth, and had seen scores of his comrades die. Few of the eventualities the SAS feared from the Iraqis arose in practice, and in view of the experiences related by the survivors of earlier wars, it

has to be said in all fairness, and without excusing them in any sense for their brutality, that in retrospect the SAS might have done far worse than to fall into Iraqi hands. If it had been the Provisional IRA into whose clutches they had fallen, it is most unlikely they would have survived.

# CHAPTER
## eighteen

THROUGHOUT MY JOURNEY IN Iraq I had been using McNab's and Ryan's books as my guides, and for the most recent phase, in Krabilah, I had relied on McNab almost exclusively. Always, though, it had seemed to me that it was Ryan's account rather than McNab's that had been closer to what I had seen and learned on the ground. Although he might have been mistaken over the fact that Phillips had compromised the patrol, he does admit that they were never really sure if the shepherd-boy had seen them. Adil – the boy himself – had told me that he had seen nothing, which contrasted sharply with McNab's story that Phillips and Coburn had actually chased after him, but was consistent with Ryan's uncertainty. Ryan's revelation that the LUP had been two kilometres away from the drop-off rather than McNab's twenty kilometres was borne out by the evidence I had amassed, and although

Ryan's description of the firefight did not tally entirely with what Abbas had told me, the idea that the patrol simply dropped their Bergens and bugged out rang true. It was, at least, far more in keeping with how I had been trained in the SAS than McNab's rendition of a sort of mini Charge of the Light Brigade against APCs and massed troops, screaming, 'Let's do it!' and hurling grenades. Published in 1995, two years after McNab's book, *The One That Got Away* presents Ryan as 'the true hero of the Bravo Two Zero mission'. Having not only made one of the most spectacular escape-marches in military history, walking 290 kilometres through enemy territory, mostly alone, in seven days and eight nights, on only two packets of biscuits and limited water, he had also, in the process, destroyed two vehicles, taking out a large number of troops, and had later killed two Iraqi guards, one with a knife and the other with his bare hands. As I left Krabilah behind me and headed back to the place where the patrol had split on the night of 24/25 January 1991, I closed McNab's book and opened Ryan's.

RETURNING TO THE MSR, THOUGH, I was once again faced with the mystery of its narrowness compared with Ryan's story that it was several kilometres wide at the point where they had crossed. In his book *Storm Command*, in which Ryan's story is first told, Sir Peter de la Billière also quotes Ryan as maintaining that the road was two to three kilometres wide at this point, adding, 'Chris warned everyone that they would have to make a good push to cross it, to avoid getting caught in the open by a passing vehicle.'[26] Ryan himself starts his 'good push' a full seven kilometres from the road – a rather exaggerated precaution for an exhausted patrol with two injured

men, to avoid being compromised crossing a track that was no more than five metres wide. Vince Phillips, who was suffering an agonizing leg injury, may well have been so intent on keeping up with Ryan that he failed to hear McNab's call that he was halting to try the TACBE radio beacon.

THE ESCARPMENT TO THE NORTH of the MSR was all buttes, dips and screes of loose rock, making it terrible going, but after a kilometre or so it evened out into the starkest plain imaginable. Not even the Arctic, I thought, could look so relentless and unforgiving as this plateau. Yet people obviously lived here. There were the dark buds of Bedouin tents on the landscape, standing out against the seams of grey-green, and even what looked like permanent farms not far away to the east. Somewhere within that wilderness ahead of me, Vince Phillips had vanished, never to be seen alive again. I had come to Iraq specifically to find out where and how he had died, but in terrain like this I knew that to pinpoint the exact spot would be well nigh impossible – Ryan's text is too vague and ambiguous for precision. I had promised the Phillips family that I would make some sort of memorial to Vince in the desert, but I did not expect to get nearer than the general area.

Days before, I had asked Abbas if he had heard of any bodies found up on the plateau at the end of January 1991 and, to my surprise, he told me of two. One corpse, he said, had consisted of little more than hands and a head – the rest of it had been eaten by wolves. The second had been discovered by a relative of his named Mohammed, about nine kilometres from his farm. Of the two cases, it was the dismembered head that interested me most. If Vince

Phillips's body had been mutilated by wolves, that might explain why the MoD hadn't allowed Jeff Phillips to see it, and why Vince's wife hadn't wanted to. But when I discovered that the head had actually been found long after January 1991, I ruled it out. I considered the second corpse a possibility, but at only nine kilometres from the LUP, it seemed too near to have been Vince. Ryan said that they had walked at least twenty kilometres from their LUP of 25 January, when Vince disappeared, and the LUP itself was a four and a half hour trek north of the MSR. Some simple mental arithmetic based on a pace of six kilometres an hour put the place at least 47 kilometres to the north.

I had asked Abbas to introduce me to Mohammed anyway, and at mid-morning on my first day back in the field, having covered about four kilometres from the MSR, I saw a Toyota pick-up moving towards me out of the heat haze. I stopped to watch it and as it pulled up I saw that there were two occupants: Abbas, and a tall, rather severe-looking Bedouin in a grey dishdasha and white shamagh. This, Abbas told me, was his relative, Mohammed, who had found the body of a soldier here on the plateau back in 1991. Mohammed was a gravel-voiced chain-smoker with a pronounced cough and rheumy, red-shot eyes who didn't look at all well. As serious and grave-mannered as Abbas was mercurial, he had been brought up here on the plateau, he said, but his father had sent him to school in al-Haqlaniya and he could both read and write. He had his own tent here with a flock of sheep, but he also had a house in al-Haqlaniya where he was employed by an oil company. I asked him if it was true that he had found a dead man here on the plateau in January 1991.

'Yes, I did,' he said. 'It was a foreign soldier in a camouflage suit. His name was Flips.'

A klaxon sounded in my head – this was simply too good to be true. I must have mentioned Vince's name to Abbas, who had passed it on to his relative, I thought. How else could Mohammed possibly have known the dead man's name was Phillips? For a moment I considered the dog-tags that all soldiers were supposed to wear on active service – these would have given name, rank, number, religion, blood group and date of birth, but they would have been in English, which Mohammed showed no sign of knowing.

'How did you know his name?' I enquired, suspiciously.

'He had two cards in his pocket,' Mohammed said without hesitation. 'With his name written in Arabic and English. The name in Arabic was "Flips". The cards offered a lot of money to anyone who helped him. But it was too late for that – he was already dead.'

I was caught completely off guard – I had forgotten about the indemnity cards the SAS patrol had been carrying. They were mentioned in passing in one of the books – whether Ryan's or McNab's, I couldn't even remember. And I was suddenly more excited than I had been since we had met Adil and Abbas: Mohammed's revelation put an entirely new complexion on things. Only an extremely detailed reading of the books could have turned up this detail, which even I had forgotten. Was I really looking at the man who had found Vince Phillips, I wondered? Had another astonishing needle in the haystack turned up?

RYAN SAYS IN HIS BOOK THAT the reason for the split was never satisfactorily explained, and states that he did not hear the aircraft for which McNab stopped to use the TACBE radio beacon, even though he can only have been a few metres from the patrol com-

mander at the time. He did not realize that the rest of the patrol had been left behind until he reached the MSR, almost an hour after he had last spoken with McNab. He waited until 0030 hours for the other five to show up, meaning he must have been at the road about midnight – according to Abbas, just as the first Iraqi troops were rolling up at the site of the firefight, only about ten kilometres away. After failing to reach McNab on the TACBE, he decided not to wait, but that the remaining three of them should press on across the plateau, stumbling about over loose stones that badly blistered their feet.

By Ryan's own reckoning, he was, by now, the only one of the three capable of making decisions. He had caught Phillips ditching ammunition he thought they might need, and had already written him off as untrustworthy. Stan was still so disoriented from his attack of heat-exhaustion that he had to be treated like a child and told to lie down whenever they halted, and when Ryan tried to get Phillips to play a part in navigating, the sergeant, he says, just nodded dumbly at anything he said. Walking close together, they continued for another four and a half hours, until the cut-off time of 0500 hours, when they began to look round for an LUP on the featureless plain. They were physically and mentally shattered, having covered at least seventy kilometres since the compromise at about 1600 hours the previous day. The only cover they could find was an old tank berm – an oval pit with six-foot walls designed to camouflage and protect a stationary tank – with deep ruts running into it. The berm was open-ended and gave no protection from the terrible wind, so instead they lay down in the half-metre deep ruts. Here, head to toe and motionless, they lay up for most of the daylight hours of 25 January.

As McNab and the other five were finding on their knoll somewhere in the desert to the west, day brought the most dreadful

conditions imaginable. By early morning it was raining, and all too quickly the rain turned to sleet and snow. Worse, while McNab's section survived by throwing caution to the wind and getting hot brews down them, huddling together for warmth, Ryan and his two comrades could do nothing but lie there. This, he says, was because daylight revealed an enemy position within six hundred metres – either a building or a box-shaped vehicle with antennae, and at least two men.

Surprisingly, the balance of survival began to change for Stan at this point – the thermal underwear that had almost killed him by dehydration during the frantic night march now kept him relatively warm and, unlike the others, he had brought with him wet rations, which he was able to swallow unheated. Vince Phillips's condition, though, started to deteriorate, and he complained continually of the cold. It was during this time, Ryan alleges, that Phillips admitted he had been aware the shepherd-boy had seen him in the LUP. Ryan had always suspected this, of course, and he cursed Vince silently, thinking that if the patrol had known for certain that they had been compromised, they could have got out of the wadi before the man on the bulldozer appeared. They might then have made a clean break back to the heli drop-off and been picked up safely (Ryan did not know at this stage that the heli had not turned up).

Ryan is clearly alleging here that Phillips was directly to blame for Bravo Two Zero's predicament, and it is significant perhaps to note that the last articulate sentences he reports from Vince sound almost like a confession of guilt.

By 1600 hours the cold had seeped so completely into their bones that, in spite of the enemy only six hundred metres away, they were obliged to cuddle up together for body warmth. When it started to

get dark they crawled into the berm and tried to run about to get their circulation going. It was only then that Ryan realized how bad their physical condition was – their hands were so stiff they were unable to hold their weapons properly and Phillips said that he could no longer carry his M16. He handed it over to Stan, who had no weapon, which left Vince with only his 9mm Browning pistol. By the time full darkness had come, they were on their way.

Ryan declares that his recollections of the events of the next few hours are hazy because he was suffering from exposure. What he does make clear is that as they marched on through the blizzard, Phillips lagged further and further behind the other two. He began to beg them to slow down, Ryan says, mumbling that he was tired and wanted to go to sleep – typical symptoms of advanced hypother-mia. Alternating between angry retorts and encouragement, Ryan kept him moving, but was pulled up short at one point when Phillips claimed that his hands had turned black. Thinking it was frostbite, Ryan examined them, only to find that Phillips was wearing black leather gloves. The sergeant's behaviour became increasingly erratic as the hours passed, and at another time he began screaming out loud, risking compromise by anyone within several hundred metres. Stan told him to shut up.

Ryan was acting as scout, marching on a bearing directed by Stan behind him who guided him left or right, though they were meandering badly. They stopped for a short break and realized sud-denly that Phillips was no longer with them. They shouted out his name and when there was no answer they backtracked, following their own footprints, which were easy to spot where the snow had piled up. After twenty minutes, Ryan says, he recognized that the task was useless. Vince Phillips had gone, and whether he had walked

off east, west, or south, or just lain down and drifted off to sleep in a hollow, they were never going to find him. Ryan decided that they should simply turn around and go on without him – if they spent any more time looking in these conditions, then they would soon both be dead. So, 'With heavy hearts,' Ryan says, 'we turned round and cracked on again and left Vince on his own.' [27]

Those last words suggest that at this point Ryan was, to some extent, optimistic about Phillips's chances of survival. They obviously exclude the idea that Phillips was anything but alive when Ryan last saw him. This uncertainty was reflected in the information given to the Phillips family back in Britain, when they were told that Vince was lost in the Gulf rather than missing, presumed dead, and is confirmed by a letter the CO of 22 SAS sent Vince's wife, in which he speaks of a foreboding of Vince's death which was only proved right when his body arrived back in Hereford. The CO's foreboding indicates clearly that there was no official presumption of Vince's death, and this uncertainty can only have originated from the people who last saw him alive – either Ryan or Stan, or both.

According to McNab, though, when he and Stan encountered each other in the Baghdad holding centre, McNab enquired about Vince, only to be told, 'Vince is dead. Exposure.' Clearly Stan, for one, does not seem to have been in any doubt about Vince's fate.


I ASKED MOHAMMED IF HE COULD show me where he had found the body.

'Yes, of course,' he said. 'It isn't far from here.'

We all piled into the pick-up and Mohammed wheeled round and headed east. Although he slowed down a couple of times, he

178

never erred from his course, and as he drove I noticed that his eyes flicked constantly from the ground to the horizon and back – just as I had seen Bedouin guides and trackers do for years. But while most deserts have at least some landmarks – a knoll, a ridge, a sequence of dunes – this place appeared to be as homogenous as an ocean. Suddenly he stopped the car and we got out. 'This is it,' he said, pointing to a patch of ground that looked exactly like all the other patches of ground. 'This is where I found him.'

It seemed so impossible that I was tempted to laugh. I knew from experience, of course, that some Bedouin were brilliant trackers. I had known Bedouin who could ride their camels a thousand miles navigating by sun and stars and never vary more than two degrees from true. I had heard of famous Arab guides who were totally blind, but could navigate with perfect precision by the direction of the wind on their faces and by feeling the varying textures of the desert surface, for which there are scores of different adjectives in Arabic. I had met Bedouin who could not only tell you almost everything about a camel from its tracks, including to whom it belonged, where it was going and when, but who could also remember every camel track they had ever seen in their lives. I knew that there was nothing mystical about this. Power of observation was a quality prized by the Bedouin – it was something that they began to learn naturally as small children and which was reinforced by years upon years of familiarity. I had travelled with Egyptian caravaneers who had been bringing back rock salt from the same oasis in the Sudan three or four times a year since they were ten years old. By the time they were forty they had covered hundreds of thousands of miles by camel in the same area, and literally knew every stone and every bush of a region that, to outsiders, looked as hostile as Mars. While

this plateau was a wilderness to us, for people like Abbas and Mohammed, it was familiar. They had grown up here, and their ancestors had lived here back countless generations to those Amorites who had wandered this plateau before the pyramids were built in Egypt. There was not a single square foot of this desert that had not once been the site of a Bedouin tent – a home where, over the centuries, tens of thousands of men and women had been born, lived out their lives and died. What the Bedouin saw when they looked at this desert was not emptiness, but a land littered with memories and peopled with ghosts.

Despite knowing all this, Mohammed's certainty amazed me. I scanned the horizon, wondering how he could be so sure. The Bedouin farms I had seen before now stood to the south of us, and to the east there were a few limestone boulders. Apart from that there was nothing – only the endless desert and the sky.

'How can you be so certain this is the place?' I asked him. 'It looks like everywhere else.'

He shrugged. 'I know this plateau,' he said.

This was the clincher. I was aware that when a Bedouin said he 'knew' a place, he didn't mean, as we might, that he had visited it once or twice. He meant much more what a London taxi driver means when he says he knows the city, only more so. It meant that he knew every inch of the place – every pebble, burrow and blade of grass – so well, indeed, that he could find his way around it on a pitch-dark night. I surveyed Mohammed's grave face and I knew instinctively that he was telling the truth: against all the odds, I had found the actual spot in the desert where Vince Phillips had died. 'I think you had better tell me from the beginning,' I said.

# CHAPTER
# nineteen

'ALL RIGHT,' MOHAMMED BEGAN. 'It was January, 1991 – ten years ago, during the war. I don't remember the exact day, but it was near the end of the month, and I remember it was unusually cold – the cold of death. I was coming from al-Haqlaniya to visit my relatives on the plateau, driving my pick-up, the same red pick-up I have now. I was coming from the north towards this spot and I saw something lying in the desert from some way off. I could tell it wasn't a sheep or a cow, and I knew it must be a human being. That was strange because it was so cold that no one would go out on foot. When I got up close and stopped I saw that it was a foreign soldier in camouflage. I realized what he was at once, because I had heard about the shooting down at Abbas's house a day or so earlier so I was sort of on the look-out.'

'Can you describe the man you found?'

'Yes. He was a strong-looking man, very tall, with long legs. To give you an idea how tall he was, I had to bend his body to get it into the back of my pick-up. He had curly hair and a moustache that curled round his mouth, and he was wearing camouflage, with boots, and on his head a big shamagh with the ends crossed over his chest. He was also wearing gloves – black leather gloves with sleeves of grey wool up his arms, and a military belt with pouches on it.'

I took out my copy of *Bravo Two Zero*, which included mugshots of the three dead members of the patrol, Consiglio, Lane and Phillips. 'Is the man you found here?' I asked Mohammed.

He peered at the pictures. It must have been difficult, for all three photos were the same size, and all three men were dressed in camouflage and had moustaches and stubbled jaws. Finally he pointed at the picture of Vince. 'It was him,' he said.

'Okay,' I said. 'What did you find on him apart from the cards?'

'In his belt he had two grenades, a bayonet, some biscuits in transparent paper and some jam in a tube. He had a water-bottle with some water in it, a mug and a pair of small binoculars. In his pockets I found two glass phials of what must have been medicine, a wallet with seventy dollars and some Saudi money, a compass and a photo of a woman – I suppose his wife – and two children.'

I stopped him there, aware that this was a crucial point. The items Mohammed had listed as being on Vince up to now had been to some extent predictable to anyone familiar with the SAS, but a photograph was not. It was strictly against standard operating procedures for anyone on patrol behind enemy lines to carry such a photo, as it could be used as a lever by interrogators in the event of capture. But what was most interesting was that while Mohammed had said two children, Ryan had written incorrectly in his book that

Vince had had three children, and McNab had not mentioned the number at all – or even that Vince was married. I knew, of course, that Vince did have two children, but this was certainly a fact no one could have found out simply by reading the books.

'Were the children boys or girls or one of each?' I asked.

Mohammed thought for a moment. 'It seemed to me they were both girls,' he said. Correct. Vince had had two daughters, Sharon and Lucy, aged six and four at the time of his death.

'You say you searched him,' I went on. 'Did you find any marks on his body – anything to indicate how he'd died?'

'There were no bullet-wounds, if that's what you mean. No blood. Like I said, I didn't take his clothes off, but there was nothing visible to me. I assumed that he'd died of the cold. It was horrendously cold here during those few days – I mean absolutely deadly cold. Why, even a Bedouin died up here around the same time. He was returning home one night when his car broke down and he tried to walk back. Froze to death on the way. And he knew the country and was wearing a really warm sheepskin coat – no wonder a foreigner who didn't know the desert should die of cold. By God, he must have been incredibly tough just to get this far with no shelter and dressed like he was.'

As we had been talking, groups of local Bedouin had wandered over in pick-ups and trucks from the nearby cluster of farms to see what was going on. Bearded, earthy-looking men in dishdashas and red-speckled headcloths, they listened gravely to what Mohammed had to say, but were evidently familiar with the story – another reason to believe it, I thought. Remembering that Ryan had mentioned a possible building not far from the berm where the SAS had spent 25 January, I wondered if he might have mistaken the farms of these Bedouin

for an enemy position. They told me, though, that the farms – actually it was a single farm with several buildings – had been built since 1991, and that there had been nothing on the same site previously.

I turned my attention back to Mohammed and asked what he had done with Vince's body. 'I put it in the back of the pick-up as I said,' he told me. 'I had to open the tailgate and bend him over to get him in. I took him to the police HQ at Rumadi, but they said they had no vehicles and asked me to take the body to Habbaniya where there was a proper morgue with a refrigeration plant. I took him there after I had handed the cards and the other things over to the Rumadi police. I was tempted to keep the money, but I looked again at the photo of his wife and children and I felt guilty and didn't. I kept the binoculars, though, because after all they were no good to him any more and I knew they would be useful in the desert. I still have them, but they're broken – my children played with them, you know.'

'Could I see them?' I asked.

'Yes, certainly, but they are at my house. I'll have to bring them later.'

Turning my mind to objects, I suddenly realized that there was something I had missed – or rather, several things. Mohammed had never mentioned the pistol Vince had been carrying, nor any ammunition. Neither had he mentioned twenty gold sovereigns, or Vince's dog-tags. When I asked him about the pistol and ammunition, he began to cough nervously. 'I never found any weapon or bullets,' he snapped.

'Come on,' I said. 'This man was a soldier. He must have had a weapon and ammunition.'

'I said there weren't any.' His manner had changed so abruptly

that I knew he was hedging. The more I pressed him, the more aggressive he became, and he began looking around for a way of escape. I sensed that he knew about the pistol; in fact I guessed he had kept it and didn't want to tell me. I decided that it would do no good to press him further about it and turned instead to the dog-tags and the gold. He heaved an audible sigh of relief. He hadn't found any gold on Vince, he told me, neither had he found any dog-tags. His voice had regained conviction and I was inclined to believe him this time. After all, he had admitted keeping Vince's binos, because they were no good to him any more, but had returned his money out of guilt. In any case, he hadn't stripped Vince's body and since the sovereigns were concealed around his waist, it was perfectly possible he hadn't found them. The dog-tags would have been around his neck, though, and easy to find. They would have had no value to Mohammed, and therefore there would have been no motive for his denying that he'd found them. Yet he insisted Vince had not been wearing dog-tags.

The dog-tags remained a mystery, but the pistol did not. That evening, Abbas took me aside and told me, 'Mohammed has the pistol. I know he has because I have seen it. He took the pistol and the ammunition, but he didn't want to admit it.'

'Why?' I asked. 'He admitted taking the binoculars.'

'Yes, but that was different. He doesn't want to admit in front of government people that he took a firearm, which would be illegal.'

It made sense, but though I subsequently tried to persuade Mohammed to show me the pistol privately, he declined.

By the time I had finished questioning Mohammed, there were at least eight or nine Bedouin around us, which made my next proposal rather awkward. I was satisfied now that I really had found

the spot where Vince had died, and I wanted to carry out my undertaking to the Phillips family to build some kind of memorial here. The obvious thing was a cairn – a fairly common feature in most deserts – but I wondered how these locals would react to the idea of building a memorial in their back garden to an enemy soldier who had also been a Christian. When I explained what I wanted to do, there was silence for a moment.

'Why not?' Abbas said. 'He deserves it.'

'Yes,' one of the Bedouin agreed. 'He was a very brave man to come here far from his own country.'

'They were all brave,' another said. 'They were real men, those soldiers, to have endured the conditions here in winter. Heroes every one.'

The rest of the Bedouin mumbled in agreement and I felt humbled. McNab had called them ragheads, but I knew this was as fine a tribute to the SAS as I was ever likely to hear.

There were no stones in the place I wanted to build the cairn, but the Bedouin knew where to get them. We jumped into Mohammed's pick-up and drove about a kilometre to the outcrop of limestone I had seen from some distance away. The Bedouin helped me pile the stones into the back of the truck and soon we were roaring back to the site of Vince's death. Before building the cairn itself, I had one more task to perform. I took out a small can of Guinness I had brought from Britain – Vince's favourite tipple – and while the Bedouin watched in surprise, I buried it in the earth, where the cairn was going to be. Then the men helped me pile the rocks and boulders over it and stood back. For a moment no one spoke. The sun was going down: a vast globe of lemon light balanced on the world's edge. A slight breeze fluttered the Bedouins' dish-

dashas, but the desert was utterly silent. This place has already become a sacred site, I thought, and thanks to all the Bedouin who had gathered here, the story of Vince Phillips would blend into local tradition, becoming part of the landscape, a legend that would be handed down among the desert people for generations. Just as the spirits of their ancestors still lived here among them, so Vince's voice would be here for ever, in the wind that drifted across the plateau. Building this cairn had been a simple act, but a satisfying one. I had proved to my own satisfaction that Vince had not compromised the Bravo Two Zero patrol. He had done his job, and no one could ask for more. I hoped this cairn would itself become part of the landscape and remain here for ever in memory of a brave British soldier who had given his life for his country – Sergeant Vincent David Phillips, of A Squadron, 22 SAS.

# CHAPTER
# twenty

FINDING THE SITE OF VINCE'S death was a tremendous advantage to me because, like the first LUP, the spot was a fixed anchor point from which I could work both backwards and forwards. This was important, for while I had found the place, and probably the cause, of Vince's death, I had not yet ascertained the circumstances. That night we were invited to the Bedouin farm for dinner, and our hosts, who belonged to the Duleim tribe, slaughtered sheep for us. Once again a vast number of guests popped up out of the desert, and after we had gorged ourselves and were sat drinking tea, there was a lot of banter. Abbas was ribbed ceaselessly as 'the one who caused the problem in the first place', and at one point a row broke out between the Bedouin and Abu Omar, the sour-faced military minder, who declared that the SAS patrol had been 'cowards who ran away from two boys and an old man'. It did my heart good to

see the Duleim tribesmen throwing down their headcloths and declaring angrily that the government representative didn't know what he was talking about. These people had to dice with the conditions Bravo Two Zero had encountered here their entire lives and understood instinctively that the true heroism the patrol had showed was not in gunning down countless men, but in surviving the appalling enemy of this desert in winter.

At one point during the evening there was a touching ceremony when Mohammed handed over to me Vince Phillips's binoculars. I looked at them carefully – they were badly broken, and although they were olive-green in colour, they were certainly not identifiable as British army issue. I remembered, though, that Ryan had made a reference in his book to members of the patrol buying pairs of little binoculars in Abu Dhabi before the operation, which he described as a distinct asset. Surely, I thought, this tended to support Mohammed's claim that the binos had belonged to the dead Vince.

Afterwards, I asked him if he knew of any tank berms in the area, hoping to find Ryan's LUP of 25 January. He looked puzzled and began to ask the others, 'What does he mean?' Nobody seemed to know, so I explained that I was looking for a sort of hole in the ground where the British soldiers might have hidden. Mohammed's face suddenly cleared. 'I know the place,' he said. 'The place I found tracks the day after I took Flips to the morgue – but it wasn't anything to do with tanks. It was a water catch-basin the Bedouin dug with a bulldozer.'

'You mean you returned to the area after you'd taken Phillips's body away?'

'Yes, because I thought there might be more of these men about. I saw tracks by Flips' body the day before and I knew he hadn't been

alone. I returned with five other people – my relatives, mostly.'

Ever since arriving on the plateau I had wondered why tanks would be in place up here when they were needed at the front in Kuwait, and the idea that the 'tank berm' was a catch-basin for the Bedouin seemed to make more sense. The next morning, soon after first light, we headed out to see the 'berm' in Mohammed's pick-up. As we drove, I asked Mohammed if there were many such basins around here. 'No,' he said. 'This is the only one I know of. We haven't dug any in recent years because of the drought. Actually, there isn't much of it left now because it has been filled in by rain and snow over the years, but at the time I found Flips – ten years ago – it was quite deep.'

He stopped the car surprisingly soon after starting off and showed me a oval-shaped hollow, no more than a foot deep, but partly surrounded by what had obviously once been high banks of spoil. It wasn't much to look at, but it was clearly the remains of some sort of earthwork, and I for one hadn't come across anything else like it in the area. Surely, I thought, this had to be it.

'So you came here the day after you found Phillips?' I asked Mohammed.

'Yes,' he said. 'I returned with five other men and we followed the tracks back from the place I found the body. It was very muddy then, and the tracks were clear. I could tell they weren't the tracks of locals. Anyway, when we arrived we found a lot of scuff marks around the water-basin – signs that people had been here, not just passing by, but had spent some time here. There were quite deep ruts leading up to the pit and there were a lot of marks around them too. The tracks led off north directly towards the place where I had found the body.'

I looked around and noticed that the Duleim houses where we had had dinner were in clear sight, not much more than a kilometre away to the east. I wondered again if they or their predecessors could have been mistaken by Ryan for a military post. This was crucial, I realized, because it was the apparent proximity of the military post (or vehicle) which had prevented the SAS men from cuddling up, getting on a hot brew or moving around, any or all of which actions might have saved Vince's life. Ryan even emphasizes in his book how Vince asked him if they could cuddle up together, to which Ryan replied that it was 'too dangerous to move'.

Mohammed confirmed that there had been no houses in that spot in 1991, and as for a military post, there never had been one here, he said. The nearest military installation was the now-ruined one I had seen while following in the footsteps of McNab, more than fifteen kilometres away. That couldn't even be seen from the berm.

What about a military vehicle?

'There was no military vehicle here then,' Mohammed said emphatically. 'I was here at the time, and I would either have seen it or seen its tracks. Nothing can pass through here without the Bedouin knowing. There was no military post and no vehicle, and no house that could have been mistaken for one.'

What surprised me about the berm was that it was so close to the road – no more than ten kilometres away. This was astonishing, because Ryan says that they left the road at about 0030 hours on 25 January and not arrived here until 0500 hours – four and a half hours' march to cover ten kilometres. When I looked closely at Ryan's map, the LUP of 25 January appeared to be only about ten kilometres north of the road, suggesting strongly that this could be the spot. And if it was, I could make a good assessment of the distance Ryan

actually covered on the night of 24/25 January. Disregarding his own map, he writes that they had covered sixteen kilometres southwards from the LUP, then ten kilometres west, then another ten to fifteen kilometres north back to the road. At the most generous estimate, then, his group had covered only forty kilometres by midnight on 24 January from the original lying up place, in roughly eight hours, rather than the sixty de la Billière reports in his account. This would, incidentally, mean that they were walking not at the nine kilometres per hour Ryan says, but at five kph – the standard SAS pace for an unladen patrol in good conditions.

If the lying up place of 25 January was only ten kilometres north of the road, then even giving Ryan's recorded figures the benefit of the doubt, his group covered only fifty kilometres that night, rather than the seventy he says. Judging by his map, though, the distance may have been even less – perhaps no more than forty. Anyone who has tried to march forty kilometres at night over rough and unknown country carrying thirty kilos will recognize that this was no mean feat. To have covered seventy, or indeed, the 'two marathons' as McNab says they did, beggars belief. Incidentally, if Ryan did cover fifty kilometres that night in eleven and a half hours, then the average pace was 4.3 kph – one which most SAS men would recognize as pretty good, given the execrable conditions.

My next task was to measure the distance between the berm and the place where Mohammed had found Vince's body. I asked Mohammed to take me back to where we had built the cairn, walking in a straight line. Although I couldn't see the little pile of stones from the berm itself, it very quickly came into focus in the flat desert. There was no mistaking the reading on my GPS. The place Vince had died was exactly three kilometres from the berm. I checked it

over and over again, but there could be no possible doubt. It was three kilometres from where Ryan and the others had lain up to the place they had lost Vince. At the pace they had been going on the previous night, that would have made it under an hour's journey, but taking into account that they were suffering profoundly from hypothermia, it might have been an hour and a half. Yet Ryan states baldly in his book that they covered forty kilometres that night and lost Vince after twenty. I had already noticed that, since the Krabilah road lay only sixteen kilometres north of the berm, it would put Vince's disappearance north of that road, when Ryan states it was to the south of it. But more than this, Ryan clearly gives the idea in his book that Vince's decline was a gradual process that continued over hours as they tried in vain to encourage him onwards, with ever-diminishing success.

If Vince had gone within an hour or so of setting off, it immediately threw the whole affair into a very different light. It even meant that the date given on Vince's headstone in St Martin's churchyard in Hereford – 26 January 1991 – was probably wrong.

Ryan says they left the berm at about 1830 hours, so if my information was correct, the time of Vince's collapse – or at least his disappearance – cannot have been after about 2000 hours on 25 January. If what Mohammed had told me was true, then Ryan must have been extremely confused about the events of that night, because even the facts he reported to the Regiment were wrong. This is borne out by the Commanding Officer's official letter to Mrs Phillips informing her of Vince's death, stating that he had wandered off in the 'course of the night and had died on the night of 25/26 January. This information, which can only have come from Ryan, suggests that the disappearance of Vince Phillips had occurred well

into the night's march, rather than a mere three kilometres – 1.8 miles – from the starting point. Ryan did apparently tell the Phillips family that Vince had died on the night of 25 January – why, then, does the headstone bear the date 26 January?

The only other versions of what happened that night come from McNab and de la Billière. Both probably originate from Ryan or Stan, and are therefore interesting for the extra details they put in or leave out. McNab, for instance, says that at one point when they stopped Vince had become incoherent, and Stan and Ryan tried to huddle around him to give him body heat, but without much success. He implies that they were walking together until they started to ascend a gradient, when Stan stopped to wait for Vince, but Vince didn't appear, whereupon both of them went back to look for him. De la Billière's account differs only in one significant detail: he reports that Ryan left Stan and went back to look for Vince alone. Both accounts are wrong in at least one aspect – Ryan and Stan could not have been climbing a gradient when Vince disappeared, since in the area where Mohammed found Vince's body there are no gradients: the desert here is completely and utterly flat. McNab himself repeats the intelligence brief the patrol were given before the mission, stating that within seventeen kilometres of the original MSR, the land dropped no more than fifty metres.

If Stan and Ryan abandoned Vince to die alone and cold as Stan has now admitted, then, of course, they had had no choice. Militarily, they had done the right thing. The great weakness of all Special Forces operations has always been the problem of casualties. The official doctrine is simply to leave them, but there is also an unwritten code of comradeship in the army obliging men to save their comrades if there is the slightest chance. There could be no moral

condemnation of Ryan and Stan. Had they not abandoned him, they would all have died.

It struck me suddenly that Ryan had felt intensely guilty about Vince's death. Even after he returned to Britain he admitted that thoughts about Vince plagued him, and he continually went over the things he might have done to save him.

Ryan must have known when writing his book that his condemnation of Vince was a breach of Regimental tradition, yet he adamantly followed it through. The other members of the patrol were obviously furious at his portrayal of Vince, because, following the TV version of *The One That Got Away*, the Phillips family received letters from Coburn, Dinger and McNab, all criticizing Ryan in no uncertain terms. 'At no time throughout the patrol did Vince display the actions portrayed . . .' Coburn wrote. 'On the contrary, the very fact that he was in the patrol disputes Ryan's version of events, otherwise he would never have been allowed to deploy across the border . . . although I did not know Vince well, I found him of immense help to me personally on the build-up to the operation. His strength of character and Regimental experience was a constant source of confidence. His actions on the ground can only be described as professional and you . . . have every right to be justly proud of him.' [28]

Stan later told the *Daily Mirror*, "What gives me the greatest pain is how Vince's death was written about by Chris Ryan. Any one of us could have dropped first. It just happened to be Vince. But to say, as Ryan did, that he wasn't up to it was despicable – utterly despicable – and the whole Regiment thought it and still thinks that."

Dinger characterized his reaction to the portrayal of Vince by Ryan as 'shock, anguish, loathing' and called it a pack of lies. 'If you can draw any comfort from this letter,' he told Veronica and her

husband, 'it is that I tell you the truth. Vince was a good mate and a key member of the patrol in a difficult situation. Vince DID NOT compromise the patrol or behave in the manner portrayed. It was an honour to have known Vince and served with him on operations.' [29]

In a letter to Vince's father, McNab confirmed that Vince had done his job proficiently and attacked Ryan bitterly for denigrating 'comrades who would have sacrificed their lives for his had the situation demanded it'. [30]

Despite these reassurances from other patrol members, there was still the classified SAS report about Vince which had been leaked to the *Mail on Sunday* that appeared to have given official sanction to Ryan's story. A close scrutiny of the report, though, leaves little doubt as to its source. Since McNab does not say that Vince alerted the herdsboy by moving, and Dinger expressly denied it, surely this allegation can only have come from Ryan himself. Similarly, the allegation that Vince fell asleep on stag is only mentioned by Ryan, and the assertion that his 'heart wasn't in it and he lacked the will to survive' is similar in form and content to Ryan's book. As he was officially second-in-command of Vince's half-patrol, Ryan would have been the proper source for such a report.

The more I thought about it, the more certain I was that Ryan's last conversation with Vince, lying in the ruts by the berm, slowly freezing to death, might provide a key. Here Ryan says that Vince confessed to the fact that he had spotted the herdsboy, and that the herdsboy had therefore seen him, confirming Ryan's view that the sergeant had jeopardized the entire mission. One of the reasons that Vince was suffering so badly from hypothermia was because – on his own admission – Ryan had refused to allow them to break hard routine, as McNab had done, and risk compromise by the enemy

position six hundred metres away. Yet by making hot brews and risking compromise, McNab had put the lives of his men higher than tactical considerations. And my eyewitness said there was no enemy position nearby, so Ryan's refusal to relax is questionable, considering Vince's condition.

Could it be, I wondered, that Ryan felt so deeply guilty for his refusal to abandon hard routine, even though according to my witness there had been no enemy nearby, that when it came to writing his book he was compelled to try to persuade his readers – and perhaps even himself – that he was not really responsible for what happened to Vince?

# CHAPTER
# twenty one

THE KRABILAH ROAD WAS ONLY sixteen kilometres north of Vince's cairn and as I came off the roof of the plateau and began to descend into the more broken country beyond, I saw the line of pylons that Ryan mentions running parallel with the asphalt road. This confirmed my belief that Vince's disappearance could not have occurred twenty kilometres north of the berm as Ryan says, because he also recalls that as he and Stan descended from the 'cruel, high plateau' he hoped to God that Vince was doing the same.

I followed their progress under the pylons and across the road towards the two-metre chain-link fence sealing off the railway line. The fence looked impenetrable from a distance, though Ryan wrote that if they had not been in such a weakened condition they would have scaled it in a minute. As it was, they had to cut their way through with a Leatherman. I had one with me and would have like to have

done the same, but my minders were waiting on the other side and I thought it inadvisable to start cutting up government property. It was only when I got right up close that I saw it would not be necessary – the fence was only nominal, riddled with gaps and holes, and I passed through without even breaking step.

I was fairly sure that I was on Ryan's and Stan's line of march on the night of 25/26 January. Ahead of me, beyond the railway line, was a round-topped hill, perhaps the very same one on which Ryan had seen anti-aircraft gun-emplacements. A few kilometres further on the land broke up into a moonscape of serried ridges, bronze-green in colour and penetrated by the deeper green veins of wadis filled with low scrub. It was in one of these wadis that the two of them had holed up at about 0530 hours on the morning of 26 January, wrapping their arms round each other for warmth.


WHEN AT MID-MORNING THE SUN broke out of the clouds, Ryan realized that it was going to be a fine day and said a silent prayer of thanks. The sunshine saved their lives. One more day in the kind of conditions they had endured in the berm would certainly have seen them off, he thought. The relative warmth of the day revived them and, to restore morale, they began cleaning their weapons and laying their kit out to dry. At about noon, they heard goats approaching and saw to their dismay that the animals were accompanied by a young shepherd, who sat down to watch his flock. Ryan was all for 'doing' the Arab if he came in their direction, but Stan demurred – he thought the shepherd might be able to help them get a vehicle and food. The argument was cut short when the man approached them abruptly and, according to Ryan, Stan jumped

up and grabbed him. He seemed innocuous enough – Ryan suspected that he was of low intelligence – but Stan began drawing pictures in the air and repeating 'house' and 'car', to which the man nodded and jabbered in Arabic. Impulsively Stan decided to go off with the man in the hope of getting hold of a vehicle. Ryan thought the proposal ridiculous, even stupid, but Stan was set on the idea, and was even prepared to leave his weapon behind to cut a less aggressive figure. Eventually Ryan let him go, on the understanding that he would wait here in the wadi until last light – about 1830 hours – and if Stan failed to return, he would press on alone. Stan had already started off with the Arab when Ryan called him back and insisted that he took his weapon. Once again he tried to persuade his comrade to shoot the Iraqi, but Stan replied that he trusted him. Taking his M16 but leaving his webbing, he set off east with his new companion. Ryan watched the two of them until they disappeared, swallowed up by the landscape. He was not to see Stan again until after the war.

RYAN AND MCNAB'S BOOKS BOTH contain short descriptions of Stan's last few hours of freedom gleaned from personal contact and the official debrief after the war. Stan's own account was included in a television documentary first transmitted in February 2002. Ryan wrote that Stan had walked for about four hours with the goatherd until, in the distance, they had seen a group of buildings with vehicles parked outside. The man had pointed to them and turned away, leaving Stan to approach them alone. As he had neared the houses, an Arab in a white dishdasha had emerged and Stan had tried to engage him in conversation. The man had made a dive

for the vehicle – a Toyota Land-Cruiser – and, thinking he was going for a weapon, Stan shot him down. The sound of the gunshot brought about eight militia-men armed with AK47s charging out of the building, and Stan blasted away at them, taking out two, until his ammunition ran out. He made an attempt to get into the Land-Cruiser, but while he was fumbling for the key, the windscreen was smashed in and he found himself staring up the barrel of a Kalashnikov. Firing wildly into the air, the Iraqis bundled him into another car and drove him to the nearest town, where he was questioned by officers and given tea. Later, though, he was starved, blindfolded, and beaten so badly he sustained a hairline fracture of the skull. Eventually he was reunited with McNab and Dinger in a holding-centre in Baghdad.

Stan's account of his capture by the Iraqis, as portrayed in the television reconstruction, was broadly similar. However, the version of events that McNab says Stan told him when they met is basically the same, but differs in some details. McNab reports, for example, that it was the shepherd – an old man, in this version – who volunteered to take them to a house and a vehicle, drawing pictures in the sand. While in McNab's account it is clear that Stan intended to hijack a vehicle, return with it and make a dash for the Syrian border that night, Ryan's account is far more ambiguous. Although Stan does talk about getting a tractor, Ryan repeats that he is convinced the Iraqis wouldn't help. He likened their situation to two German paratroopers dropped in the UK during World War Two – any British civilian offering assistance would only be doing so as a ruse, 'to put us in the nick', as Ryan wrote. At one stage Ryan apparently tells his mate, 'It'll mean us splitting up,' – an almost subliminal indication that he knew his friend would not return. In McNab's

text it is a hut rather than a group of buildings that the shepherd guides Stan to, and a soldier rather than a civilian in a white dish-dasha whom the SAS man drops. A group of six or seven more soldiers then runs out, and Stan gets off three shots, hits two of the squaddies, gets a stoppage and runs to the car, where he is brought up sharply by a rifle in the ribs.

I HAD ASKED ABBAS IF HE KNEW of any isolated cottage, hut or group of buildings in the desert nearby, and once again he came up trumps. As I camped that night on the side of a broad wadi, he turned up and told me that there was only one such house that he knew of – about ten kilometres from here and twelve from the main road leading to Ani, the nearest small town. The house was uninhabited now, but was owned by a man from his own tribe called al-Haj Abdallah, an educated person who lived in Ani, but who owned a large flock of sheep. Abdallah, he told me, knew about the capture of a British commando here in 1991. Not only was this Abdallah a distant relation of Abbas's, but he had also encountered him in Baghdad, when he had been presented to Saddam Hussein with himself, his father, and Adnan Badawi as another citizen who had helped foil the commando patrol which had been dropped on Iraqi soil.

That night Abbas and I talked for several hours by the fire. He told me of his years in the Special Forces during the Iran-Iraq war – how he had been terrified of dying until he had dreamed of his grandfather, who had told him not to be afraid. He described the incidents in which he had been wounded, horrific accounts of hand-to-hand fighting, and told me how he had come face to face with an Iranian in no-man's land. 'He was a big fellow,' he said. 'And I was

202

out of ammunition and so was he. He pulled a grenade out, so I jumped on him and hit him a great wallop with my rifle-butt. When he went down, I picked up a stone and kept on bashing and bashing him with it till he let out a long "aaaaaaargh". God forgive me, but it was him or me. Another time I was crawling over a ridge with a friend and the Iranians opened up on us with machine-guns. A bullet hit my helmet and knocked me out and my friend carried me back to our lines. He got a citation for that.

'God knows, I have been near to death many times and now I don't fear it any more. You only fear death if you are attached to the things of life. I love my children, but I know they have only been lent to me by God for a time and aren't my possessions. The same with money or livestock – we are only the stewards of our wealth. It doesn't belong to us but to God, and we cannot take it with us when we go. My only problem is my ankle – I can't run or walk far any more. The doctors here have no fear of God. They operated on me in Baghdad and it came out worse. Do you think I could get a better operation in Britain?'

Abbas had the qualities which I admired most in the Bedouin: their courage, endurance, hospitality, loyalty and generosity. He was a simple man with an uncomplicated outlook who had been dragged into a hellish war, had seen the worst that the modern world had to offer, but had never lost his humility. I realized, too, that Abbas was the key to the whole story – not only my own investigation, but the Bravo Two Zero story itself. Fate is a strange mistress, I thought. Andy McNab's patrol had been dropped on the doorstep of a man with twelve years' experience in Special Forces, who had spotted them and organized an attack. Everything that had happened to them had resulted from his alertness. In my story, too, he had been the

prime mover: he had introduced me to the man who had found Vince, related Adnan's story and showed me the site of the hijack. Abbas might have been 'got at' by the government, I reflected, but when you spend weeks in the desert with someone, their true character comes through, and I would have put Abbas bin Fadhil down as one of the most honest men I had ever met in my life.

'It is a sin to lie,' he told me often. 'You might get away with it, but you cannot hide from God. Lying is a terrible disgrace.'


THE HOUSE ABBAS HAD TOLD ME about lay where he had said it was, ten kilometres away – it was neither a group of buildings, nor exactly a hut, but a stone-built cottage of about four rooms standing by an ancient well on a wadi side. The roof had fallen in and the rooms were full of rubble. Abbas told me that the well had been dry for many years. I couldn't tell, of course, if there were any other cottages like this one around, but Abbas had told me there weren't, and certainly I had seen no others, nor were they marked on the map. The house was connected with the main asphalt road to Ani by a cart-track, and while I waited there in what little shade there was, Abbas went off to fetch al-Haj Abdallah.

I had a long wait. It was afternoon by the time they arrived back. Abbas introduced me to a surly, bespectacled man, who looked anything but a Bedouin. He wore a red shamagh with black cords and a gilt-edged brown cloak. Abdallah had been brought up in Ani, where he was a local party official, but had inherited a large flock of sheep, which he kept out here on the fringes of the desert. The cottage was now derelict, but in the past he had used it to house the shepherd who looked after his flock. Ten years ago, he said, it had been used by

a young shepherd whom he described as backward, which immediately struck a familiar note. Ryan had described the man whom Stan had gone off with as being of low intelligence and the village idiot. I asked avidly after this shepherd, but Abdallah said that he was no longer working for him.

We sat down in the shade and I asked Abdallah to tell me what he had seen here back in 1991. 'It was 26 January,' he said, 'and I drove from Ani in my Toyota pick-up to visit my shepherd who was then living in this cottage, to see if he needed any food or drink. When I arrived he wasn't here, but as I looked around I saw a man up in the wadi about two hundred metres away. I drove towards him and I realized he was a foreign soldier. He was carrying a rifle. I drove up and spoke to him – I know a little English – and asked him what he was doing there. I said to him that I would go to Ani and bring back food, and he seemed quite agreeable to this and didn't try to stop me. Of course, I went straight to the police in Ani and told them there was an enemy soldier near my cottage. They collected about fifteen men and set off back in Land-Cruisers.

# CHAPTER
# twenty two

RYAN WRITES THAT HE WAITED for Stan in the wadi until about 1830 hours, when he decided that his friend wasn't coming back and set off on the original bearing. He had been marching for only fifteen minutes when he saw headlights approaching the place he had just left. His first thought was that Stan had actually managed to get hold of a vehicle, but when he realized there were two sets of headlights he knew it had to be the enemy, and that Stan had been captured. The two vehicles came charging towards him in the moonlight and, according to Ryan, he found shelter behind a small bush, where he prepared to make his last stand. He didn't know, he says, if they had seen him, but he didn't want to take the risk. He had already opened up the 66mm rocket-launcher he had carried with him since the first contact on 24 January, and when the two four-wheel-drive vehicles got within twenty

metres he let the first vehicle have it with a rocket head-on.

There was a whoosh and a resounding thump as the missile struck home, and the vehicle stopped. Ryan dropped the useless 66mm tube, grabbed his M16 and smacked a 40mm grenade into the bonnet of the second vehicle. He then charged the vehicles, sprayed the men in dishdashas who were sitting in the back with bullets and then, realizing he was out of ammunition, ran away. He picked up the rest of his magazines and hared off into the desert until he could run no further, then slowed down to a walk, carrying on without a break for a further two hours.

Although this must easily have been the most dramatic action Ryan had ever been involved in in his life, he devotes only eleven lines of text to his close-quarter assault on the vehicles. He does not mention details of the drivers or passengers, saying in passing only that there were 'men in dishdashas' in the back. No images, sounds, smells or sensations are evoked whatsoever, and there is no mention of any reaction from the enemy force – not so much as a scream, even. The Arabs – who Ryan says were obviously looking for him – seem to have sat there passively like statues, without even trying to jump out, run away or fight back, while the man they had been on the lookout for had mowed them down single-handedly. Not everyone has brilliant powers of description, of course, but Ryan's do not seem to be lacking in the other parts of the book. It is not every day one knocks out two vehicles and kills a score of enemies, not even in the SAS.

Coburn, in his testimony at the Auckland trial, singled out this incident as fictitious. Coburn was not, of course, there at the time, but he certainly was present at the official debriefs afterwards, in which, according to former RSM Peter Ratcliffe, Ryan did not

mention having had contacts with any Iraqi personnel during his walk to freedom.

Ryan continued alone, coming to the Euphrates that night, where he filled his water-bottles, then he turned due west towards Syria. Moving by night, lying up by day, boxing round any obstacles, he managed to continue without food for another five days until he finally climbed across the border fence near al-Qaim in the early hours of 30 January. Earlier that night, though, he says he faced the final test of his will to survive when he was obliged to kill two Iraqis, one with a knife and the other with his bare hands. Ryan says that in the course of that night he had inadvertently walked into the middle of an Iraqi army motor-transport park surrounded by houses and full of soldiers. As he crouched in the shadows, trying to work out how to get back to the road, two men approached, and when they passed, Ryan says, his survival instinct took over and, whipping out his knife, he struck the first man in the neck and 'ripped his throat out'.[31] The other man ran off, but Ryan rushed after him, brought him down and, getting one arm round his throat in a judo hold, wrung his neck. The man died instantly.

Once again, though this is apparently the first time in his life that Ryan has ever killed men with his hands, he devotes only a paragraph to the whole incident. McNab himself has explained in his book just how difficult it is to kill a man with a knife: 'You have to get hold of his head,' he says, 'hoik it back as you would with a sheep, and just keep on cutting until you've gone right through the windpipe and the head has just about come away in your hands.' [32] Yet what impelled Ryan to go out of his way to attack these men in the first place? 'Ryan's . . . claimed actions during his E and E run,' wrote SAS veteran Ken Connor, 'were directly contrary to the stan-

dard operating procedures taught to every SAS man in combat survival training . . . Chris Ryan knew that his prime task was to protect the rest of his patrol by evading capture, yet he claims to have invited contact with the enemy by launching attacks on Iraqi sentries. Either he was badly trained, or he deliberately broke SOPs, or we must seek another reason for his version of events.'[33]

Ex-RSM Peter Ratcliffe says in his book *Eye of the Storm*: 'In the official debriefing . . . which was recorded on video,' he writes, '"Ryan" made no mention of encountering any enemy troops during his epic trek to freedom. Yet in his book there are several accounts of contacts, and even a description of an incident when he was forced to kill an Iraqi sentry with a knife. If these incidents happened, then I find it difficult to believe that they could have slipped his mind during the debriefing.'[34]


THAT NIGHT I SLEPT AT THE COTTAGE where Stan had been captured and in the morning I continued my progress towards the Euphrates, crossing undulating ground that was dotted with what looked like semi-permanent Bedouin camps. I crossed beneath the pylons under which Ryan had sat down, and the road beneath which he had lain up in a culvert. It was the early hours of the morning by the time I came to the great system of dry wadis Ryan mentions, and as I made my way through the muddy fields down by the Euphrates, the first light of dawn was already gleaming on the water. When I reached the bank I knelt down and filled my water-bottles, just as Ryan had done somewhere near here ten years earlier, and sat back to watch the sunrise. I had accounted for the death or capture of seven members of the Bravo Two Zero patrol, all

of them under different circumstances from the ones described in the books.

Ryan's fate was known. He was 'the one that got away', who had personally made SAS history by completing the longest escape march ever made by a member of the Regiment. It was a feat of human endurance and determination which has rarely been equalled – a riveting story in itself. This always had been, I thought, a story that was much more about the desert than about the Iraqis: Chris Ryan might not have killed all the Iraqi soldiers he says, but he had survived against the greater enemy, against all the odds. I had intended to complete Ryan's march to the Syrian border – easy enough in daylight, with time and logistics on my side – but suddenly I no longer had the stomach for it. There would always be the ghost of Vince Phillips. I took a long, cool drink of the ancient water of the Euphrates, just as the sun burst in all its royal fiery plumage over the distant hills.

# CHAPTER
# twenty three

THE DAY BEFORE I LEFT BAGHDAD I was taken to see some relics of the Bravo Two Zero patrol that had been arranged for a private viewing in a house in the suburbs. There were no M16s, but all four of the patrol's Minimis were there, painted camouflage colours, one of them with its top-cover smashed. This, I imagined was Stan's Minimi – the one McNab had carried until after the split, and had dismantled. There was a mass of webbing, impossible to identify – although one of the pouches contained brown waxed-paper wrappings that might have held the plastic explosive McNab had apparently been carrying when he was captured. I was also shown three of the eight Bergens the patrol had ditched when Abbas and Hayil had bumped them. The other five packs were missing, purloined by Bedouin or soldiers somewhere along the line, Abu Omar said. The three remaining packs were of the SAS type I was familiar with, one

marked 'Bob' – obviously Bob Consiglio – and another 'Lane'. This latter had been the patrol-signaller's Bergen, I thought ironically, and the one that McNab said Legs had told him was 'shot to fuck', though it was perfectly intact. The third pack had a name scrawled on it that I didn't recognize, but may have been a Bergen drawn from the stores at random before the campaign. I was disappointed not to have found Ryan's own Bergen so I could confirm that it had been struck by an S60 shell as McNab says.

This was the crowning touch on a journey that had become much more than an attempt to find out the truth about Vince Phillips: a journey that had turned into a fascinating historical detective story. If what I had discovered was correct then Vince Phillips had not compromised Bravo Two Zero. The patrol hadn't even been spotted by the herdsboy as they had surmised, but by the man on the bulldozer who had wandered into their LUP quite innocently. He had seen two men, not one, and even if one of those was Vince, Abbas had been so close to them that eluding his view would have been impossible. They had not been attacked by masses of Iraqi infantry and armour, but by three civilians. They had not charged, and they had not been shot up by S60s. They had carried 95 kilos per man not twenty kilometres over flat desert, but only two kilometres. They had not been pursued by the enemy. They had not covered the distances they claimed on the first night of the escape and evasion plan. They had not hijacked a 'New York Yellow Cab', had not had a shoot-out at the vehicle checkpoint, but had left the car before reaching it, and had had an Iraqi with them in the vehicle. McNab and Coburn had not shot up a large convoy. They had not been mistreated by their captors, at least not initially, but had been shown acts of kindness. Vince Phillips had not been responsible for

the split, nor could the cowardly behaviour ascribed to him by Ryan possibly have occurred. Vince had probably died on 25 January, not the following day. Ryan did not destroy two vehicles nor gun down their occupants. Neither did he kill any sentries with his bare hands. Finally, far from clocking up 250 Iraqis killed and injured, Bravo Two Zero did not inflict anything like the massive casualties McNab and Ryan claim in their book.


BACK IN SWINDON, I PRESENTED Vince's binoculars to the Phillips family and showed them film clips of the Iraqi Bedouin helping me to build the memorial cairn. They were delighted with the binos and moved by the fact that I had buried the can of Guinness, but greeted the participation of the Bedouin with some surprise. I understood why. The Iraqis were *the enemy* – why should they be helping to commemorate the death of a man who had gone out there to kill them? I was familiar with the Arabs and spoke their language, but for most British people, I realized, it was difficult to see past the prejudices created by years of what amounted essentially to propaganda. In the end – to people back home – my witnesses were 'ragheads', and why should anyone believe them? I was reminded of St Exupery's story in *The Little Prince* of the Turkish astronomer who discovered a new planet: the other astronomers would not accept his discovery because he wore Turkish dress.

Of course, the Iraqis might have penned the names 'Bob' and 'Lane' on the Bergens I had seen in Baghdad. In fact, the entire operation – everyone I'd interviewed and everywhere I'd visited – could have been part of a massive sting. One scenario ran like this: while I had been delayed in Baghdad on the pretext of awaiting permission

from the military, Iraqi intelligence officers had read McNab's and Ryan's books, digested the story right down to the most insignificant details, and rushed up to Anbar to brief Abbas and his brother and all his family as to what they should say. Adil, the shepherd-boy, had been instructed to say that he had not seen the patrol in the wadi. McNab says the patrol was attacked by armoured personnel carriers and large numbers of enemy troops; Abbas was to say there had been only three men. McNab says they were pursued by vehicles for many kilometres; Abbas was to tell me there had been no pursuers. McNab wrote that they hiked twenty kilometres carrying 95 kilos – fifteen stone – per man; Abbas was to say that he had heard the helicopter come in two kilometres away. Ryan asserts he was the first man in the patrol when it moved out, but Abbas was to say it was the last but one man who waved to them. Abbas was then to introduce me to Mohammed, who was also briefed to say he had found Vince's body in a certain place on the plateau, kilometres short of where it had actually been found, and give all the details of what had been in Vince's pockets – even a photo of his wife and two daughters, which the Iraqi intelligence had somehow found out, even though that was not mentioned in either of the books. Mohammed had also been told to convince me he had Vince's pistol by a cunning double-bluff, and had been given a pair of binoculars that had once belonged to Vince to emphasize his veracity. Mohammed had been obliged to show me a pit which he claimed was Ryan's 'tank berm', which happened to coincide with the point marked on Ryan's map. He and Abbas and the other Bedouin had been induced to pretend they thought the patrol were 'heroes' to prove that they had no axe to grind. The Iraqi intelligence agents would also have had to concoct a newspaper interview with Adnan Badawi and get Abbas –

whom they had got me to employ as a guide without suggesting it by making sure I got separated from the vehicles on my first day out – to tell a cock-and-bull story that Adnan had been with McNab in the car and that there had been no shoot-out at the VCP. They had also somehow found out McNab's real name, which was a closely guarded secret even from the British public. Ahmad, the police sergeant major, had been told to corroborate Adnan's story, and he and all the witnesses in Krabilah been got at in advance to present a sugar-coated version of the arrest or deaths of members of the patrol and, with the inhabitants of Rummani, had been admonished to tell me, if asked, that no Iraqis had been killed or injured.

The more I mulled over it, the more I realized that it just wouldn't wash. So many of the facts I had been presented with were totally irrelevant to Iraqi propaganda – whether Adil had or had not seen the patrol, for instance, which man had waved, or the exact location of Vince's corpse. So many other facets of the books were questionable completely independently of my Iraqi witnesses: the fact that Ryan reported that the heli drop-off was only two kilometres from the LUP, for example, or that an Iraqi had been present with McNab in the taxi; the fact that Coburn had pointed out that many of McNab's and Ryan's claims were false. The effort to assimilate all the detailed material and to concoct an alternative scenario would have just been too great a task for an intelligence service in a country exhausted by war, with a return of little value. Our film was not, after all, going to get sanctions lifted. If there were inaccuracies in what I had been told, it was much more likely that they were individual, rather than part of a conspiracy – a failure of memory here, a small prejudice there, an individual interpretation or an attempt to show oneself in a favourable light. But most of all, I didn't believe

there had been a conspiracy because over the weeks in Iraq I had come to trust Abbas – this 'idiot on the bulldozer' – as one of the wisest and most honest men I had met.

Nevertheless, I knew that many would question the statements of my witnesses, which is why my final objective was to talk to the man who had been at the very heart of SAS organization during the Gulf War: ex-RSM Peter Ratcliffe. As everyone in the army knows, the rank of Regimental Sergeant Major holds almost mystical con-notations. The RSM is a unique figure: the highest ranking non-com-missioned officer in a regiment or battalion, he generally has more experience than anyone else in the unit, including most of the officers. As there can only be one RSM at any one time, he is the symbol and embodiment of the Regiment itself.

I met Peter Ratcliffe on neutral but mutually familiar ground, in the Brecon Beacons, where both of us had trained with the Para-chute Regiment more than twenty years earlier, and where both of us had passed selection for our different SAS units. Ratcliffe was a man in his early fifties: a very fit, alert-looking individual, whose jeans were immaculate and whose walking boots were highly polished. Ratcliffe had been awarded the DCM for his role in commanding an SAS unit behind enemy lines in Iraq during the Gulf War, where he had become the only NCO in British military history to have relieved an officer of his post. He had also had the gall to hold an official meeting of the sergeants' mess in the field – the subject of the painting *Mess Meeting at Wadi Tubal* by war artist David Rowlands. Ratcliffe had remained in the army for several years after the war, and had eventually been commissioned, leaving with the rank of major. He described the transition from RSM to major as 'changing from a cockerel to a feather duster overnight'.

He had done stints with both 21 and 23 SAS and an armoured regiment before retiring.

According to his own story, when Ratcliffe was being presented with his DCM by the queen, Her Majesty commented that 'it must have been terrible in the Gulf War'. 'Actually, Your Majesty, I quite enjoyed it,' Ratcliffe replied, which immediately cut short the conversation.

Down-to-earth, frank and open, I suspected that Ratcliffe's rather stern, bluff exterior concealed a deep ability to empathize with others and an extremely high intelligence. First, I asked him about the allegations that the Bravo Two Zero patrol had been ill-prepared for the operation.

'They turned down the idea of taking vehicles,' he said. 'That, in my opinion, was their biggest mistake. Both the Boss (Commanding Officer) and I advised them strongly to do so, but McNab rejected the advice. That was really the cause of everything that went wrong. As for preparation, they had access to the same data that everyone else had at that time – no more nor less. The satellite images they had weren't the best because they didn't show depressions, but with experience McNab should have known they would be there. As far as the weather goes, the met boys predicted that it would be much milder and no one serving in the Regiment had fought in the Iraqi desert before, so we had no experience. As you know, predicting the weather is never easy – the point is that we were all in the same boat.'

I realized that, in fact, the patrol had had more detailed information than they had suggested – McNab notes that the intelligence officer who briefed the patrol told them that the desert was rocky with hardly any sand, yet he had persisted in going ahead with the

idea of digging an OP anyway. Ryan states clearly that he did not find the presence of barking dogs near the heli drop-off point unexpected because the satellite images they had been shown revealed human habitation. This negates McNab's statement that Abbas's house should not have been there. The allegation that there were more than three thousand troops in the area is unproven, and is irrelevant anyway, if Abbas's account of the firefight is correct. In the end – even if they existed – these troops did not play a part in the capture of the patrol. According to my witnesses, Consiglio was shot by civilians and the rest of the patrol were captured by civilians or police. In addition, McNab might have detected the presence of a military base – and therefore the possibility of troop concentrations and anti-aircraft defences – simply by looking at the map, on which the compound stands out 'like balls on a bulldog', as he would have put it.

'What about the fact that they were given the wrong radio frequencies?' I asked Ratcliffe.

'When a signaller is given frequencies for an operation, he is supposed to check them, and it is the patrol commander's duty to make sure he does. "McNab" wrote in his book that this was a "human error" that shouldn't happen again, but the question is, whose error? The responsibility was McNab's.'

I enquired about the allegation – particularly by Coburn – that the Regimental command had not sent an immediate rescue mission in keeping with tradition: a failure that was tantamount to betrayal.

'A helicopter did go out on 24 January,' Ratcliffe said, 'but the pilot was taken seriously ill and had to turn back. Subsequently, two rescue missions were launched – one involving both a British Chinook and an American helicopter and five members of the Reg-

iment. They searched the area where the patrol should have been and followed their probable escape and evasion route back to Saudi, at great risk to their own lives, but did not find them because they had changed their E and E plan and gone for Syria instead. McNab had written very clearly in his plan, which was submitted to Operations before the mission, that in the event of serious compromise, the patrol would head towards the Saudi border. To have changed the plan would have been fine if they had been in radio contact, but they weren't, and by changing it they were putting at risk the lives of all those involved in attempts to rescue them.'

Finally, bearing in mind what I had been told by my eyewitnesses in Iraq, I asked Ratcliffe what the patrol had said about their experiences on their return to the UK after the war, in March 1991.

'Every member of the Regiment who had been on patrol or in action during the Gulf War was debriefed on return,' he said. 'The debriefings were held in front of the whole Regiment and recorded on video. The idea was that everyone would benefit from hearing about the experiences of those who had been at the sharp end. The one jarring note is that what was said at the debrief often differs widely from what has been written in some of the books published later. When Ryan was debriefed we all marvelled at his skill, courage and endurance in walking 186 miles to safety. But he made no mention at all of encountering enemy troops on his trek. I talked to Ryan on many occasions afterwards and he never made any references to knocking out vehicles or killing men with a pocket knife or his bare hands. I personally find it puzzling that he should have forgotten that. As for McNab, he told us in the debriefing that the patrol had been involved in several minor skirmishes with the Iraqis and had returned fire. There was no mention at all of being involved in fire-

fights with hordes of enemy or extremely heavy contacts with Iraqi armoured vehicles and substantial contingents of infantry.'

Ratcliffe also said that he felt it insensitive on Ryan's and McNab's parts to hide behind pseudonyms when they named their three dead colleagues in their books, in deliberate contravention of the Regiment's traditional silence. Ratcliffe, who writes under his own name, scorns the idea that McNab uses the pseudonym for security reasons. 'Neither McNab or Ryan are serving in the Regiment any longer,' he said. 'So what possible reason could they have for concealing their true identities?'

Finally, Ratcliffe solved the mystery of Vince's missing dog-tags. 'He probably wasn't wearing any,' he said. 'I never have. Mine are still sealed in the plastic bag they were issued to me in. A lot of the lads never wear them at all.'

WHATEVER MCNAB AND RYAN WROTE, the fact is that they and their comrades survived against incredible odds. They were dropped behind enemy lines without transport in an area where concealment was nigh impossible, and yet they persisted with their mission. Once compromised, they displayed a determination and resourcefulness that was almost incredible given the terrible conditions they were obliged to work under. They gave their all, and pushed themselves to the very bounds of death – some of them beyond it. The grit and resilience they displayed in the face of overwhelming odds were in the highest traditions of the 22nd Special Air Service Regiment: the finest fighting unit in the world. As Abbas himself said, 'They were heroes. They were given an impossible job, that's all.'

Their true heroism is only marred, Ratcliffe agrees, by the dubi-

ous nature of much of what they have subsequently written. So why was the basic story not enough?

The blame must lie not with McNab and Ryan, but with us, the reading public, who demand of our heroes not endurance, but the resolution of all problems by force. In today's morality, when the response to every international threat is to hit out, force itself is viewed as cleaner and more upright than subterfuge, and aggression and violence are the defining characteristics of heroism and power. More than anything, McNab and Ryan exist to hide a truth about war that is to be found at the level of Baghdad's Amiriya Bunker: that it is a filthy business in which thousands of innocent people are mutilated and killed by faceless weapons developed and operated by tens of thousands of faceless men and women. In this age when wars are won by technology, we are more anxious than ever to believe in Rambo. But Rambo does not exist, not even in the SAS. He is a cipher – an acceptable human mask for the incomprehensible monster of modern war.

# NOTES

TOTGA: Chris Ryan *The One That Got Away* London 1995

BTZ: Andy McNab *Bravo Two Zero* London 1993

EOTS: Peter Ratcliffe *Eye of the Storm* London 2000

GF: Ken Connor *Ghost Force – The Secret History of the SAS* London 1998

SC: Sir Peter de la Billière *Storm Command* London 1992

1   McNab: in an interview with the BBC 2000

2   McNab BTZ   p30

3   McNab BTZ   p136

4   De la Billière   SC   p192

5   Ratcliffe EOTS   p191

6   Ryan TOTGA   p31

7   Ratcliffe EOTS   p230

8   Ryan TOTGA   p57

9   Ryan TOTGA   p25

10   Ratcliffe EOTS   p202

11   Ratcliffe EOTS   p203

12   Ryan TOTGA   p53

13   McNab BTZ   p41

14   Ratcliffe EOTS   p177

15   Ratcliffe EOTS   p129

16   Ratcliffe EOTS   p243

17   Connor GF   p474

18   Ratcliffe EOTS   p200

19   Ratcliffe EOTS   p200

20   Ratcliffe EOTS   p200

21   Ratcliffe EOTS   p243

22   Ratcliffe EOTS   p243

23   McNab in an interview with the BBC 2000

24   McNab BTZ   p199

25   Ryan TOTGA   p156

26   McNab BTZ   p148

27   De la Billière SC   p237

28   Mike Coburn in a letter to James Phillips 19/2/96

29   Dinger in a letter to James Phillips 19/2/96

30   McNab in a letter to James Phillips 19/2/96

31   Ryan TOTGA   p156

32   McNab BTZ   p148

33   Connor GF   p492

34   Ratcliffe EOTS   p260

# ABBREVIATIONS

AAA     Anti-aircraft guns

AK47    Aktion Kalashnikov (7.62mm assault rifle, originally Russian-made)

APC     Armoured personnel carrier

AWACS  Airborne warning and control systems

CO      Commanding Officer (in charge of large formation eg a regiment or battalion)

DCM    Distinguished Conduct Medal (awarded to non-commissioned ranks for bravery, now replaced by DSO, Distinguished Service Order, for all ranks)

FOB     Forward Operating Base (SAS HQ nearest to area of operations)

GPMG   General Purpose Machine Gun (7.62mm machine-gun with sustained fire capability)

GPS     Global Positioning System (satellite navigation device)

| | |
|---|---|
| LRDG | Long Range Desert Group (WW2 Special Forces group, immediate predecessor of SAS) |
| LUP | Lying up point |
| L2 | High explosive grenade |
| M16 | 5.56mm Armalite rifle, US made |
| M203 | 40mm grenade launcher affixed to M16 rifle |
| MSR | Main Supply Route |
| NBC | Nuclear, Biological and Chemical warfare |
| NCO | Non-Commissioned Officer |
| OC | Officer Commanding (in charge of smaller units, eg a squadron or company) |
| OP | Observation Post |
| RSM | Regimental Sergeant Major (highest non-commissioned rank in a regiment or battalion: individual responsible for discipline) |
| SBS | Special Boat Service (Royal Marines) |
| TA | Territorial Army |
| Two i/c | Second-in-Command |

# INDEX